Teach Yourself

VISUALLY™

Fashion Sewing

Teach Yourself VISUALLY™
Fashion Sewing

by Carole Ann Camp

WILEY

Wiley Publishing, Inc.

Teach Yourself VISUALLY™ Fashion Sewing

Published by Wiley Publishing, Inc., Hoboken, New Jersey

For general information on our other products and services or to obtain technical support please contact our Customer Care Department within the U.S. at (877) 762-2974, outside the U.S. at (317) 572-3993 or fax (317) 572-4002.

Wiley also publishes its books in a variety of electronic formats. Some content that appears in print may not be available in electronic books. For more information about Wiley products, please visit our web site at www.wiley.com.

Library of Congress Control Number: 2010943463

ISBN: 978-0-470-54297-2 (pbk)

ISBN: 978-0-470-88131-6 (ebk)

Printed in the United States of America

10   9   8   7   6   5   4   3   2   1

Book production by Wiley Publishing, Inc. Composition Services

Praise for the Teach Yourself VISUALLY Series

I just had to let you and your company know how great I think your books are. I just purchased my third Visual book (my first two are dog-eared now!) and, once again, your product has surpassed my expectations. The expertise, thought, and effort that go into each book are obvious, and I sincerely appreciate your efforts. Keep up the wonderful work!

—*Tracey Moore (Memphis, TN)*

I have several books from the Visual series and have always found them to be valuable resources.

—*Stephen P. Miller (Ballston Spa, NY)*

Thank you for the wonderful books you produce. It wasn't until I was an adult that I discovered how I learn—visually. Although a few publishers out there claim to present the material visually, nothing compares to Visual books. I love the simple layout. Everything is easy to follow. And I understand the material! You really know the way I think and learn. Thanks so much!

—*Stacey Han (Avondale, AZ)*

Like a lot of other people, I understand things best when I see them visually. Your books really make learning easy and life more fun.

—*John T. Frey (Cadillac, MI)*

I am an avid fan of your Visual books. If I need to learn anything, I just buy one of your books and learn the topic in no time. Wonders! I have even trained my friends to give me Visual books as gifts.

—*Illona Bergstrom (Aventura, FL)*

I write to extend my thanks and appreciation for your books. They are clear, easy to follow, and straight to the point. Keep up the good work! I bought several of your books and they are just right! No regrets! I will always buy your books because they are the best.

—*Seward Kollie (Dakar, Senegal)*

Credits

Acquisitions Editor
Pam Mourouzis

Project Editor
Suzanne Snyder

Copy Editor
Elizabeth Kuball

Technical Editor
Louise Beaman

Editorial Manager
Christina Stambaugh

Vice President and Publisher
Cindy Kitchel

Vice President and Executive Publisher
Kathy Nebenhaus

Interior Design
Kathie Rickard, Elizabeth Brooks

Photography
Matt Bowen

Illustrations
Ronda David-Burroughs, Cheryl Grubbs

Special Thanks...

To the following companies for granting us permission to show photographs of their patterns:

- Anna Maria Horner
- Figgy's
- McCall's Patterns
- Patty Young

About the Author

Carole Ann Camp started sewing costumes for her grandmother's costume shop when she was in middle school. In home economics class in seventh grade, while all the other students were learning to thread a needle and make a simple skirt, she convinced the teacher to let her make a costume of green chiffon and gold sequins. In high school, her grandmother handed her a bolt of maroon satin and said, "Here, how about a *Gone with the Wind* ball gown?" No pattern, mind you, just a bolt of fabric.

Carole Ann is the definition of a Renaissance woman. Three of her academic degrees are in science education; she also has a Master of Divinity degree. She is an ordained minister in the United Church of Christ and has served many parishes. Her hobbies include all the fiber and fabric arts—sewing, quilting, knitting, crocheting, needlepoint, and embroidery—and furthermore, she tap dances!

Acknowledgments

I want to thank the editors and illustrators at Wiley Publishing, Inc., as well as the photographers and seamstresses, without all of whom this book would never have been created and finished.

Table of Contents

CHAPTER 1   Tools and Materials

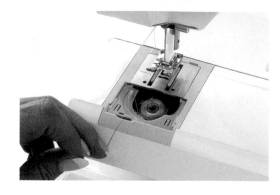

CHAPTER 2   Technique Review

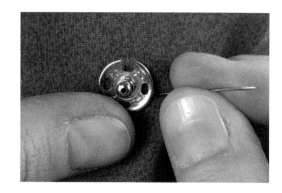

CHAPTER 3　Sewing from a Pattern

CHAPTER 4　Find the Right Fit

Table of Contents

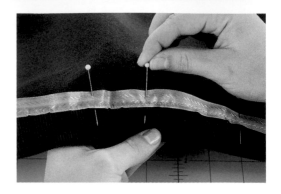

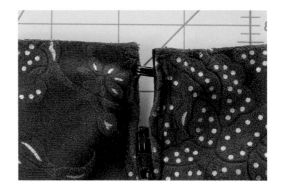

CHAPTER 7 Necklines, Armholes, and Straps

CHAPTER 8 Skirts

Table of Contents

CHAPTER 9 Pants

CHAPTER 10 Tops

CHAPTER 11 Dresses

CHAPTER 12 Recycle, Refurbish, and Repair

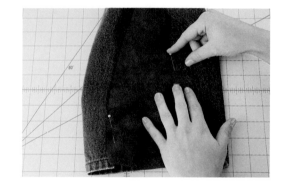

CHAPTER 1

Tools and Materials

Sewing is a practical hobby. Not only do you have the fun of being creative, but you also end up with a new garment or outfit that makes a statement about who you are—an item of clothing in the color and fabric you selected, and which really fits you, with the darts in the right place, the amount of ease you like, and the waistline and hemline exactly where you want them to be. You may experience a rush when your friends ask, "Where did you get that great dress/skirt/top?" and you answer, "I made it myself!"

There are thousands of gizmos and gadgets for home sewers on the market today, but there are only a few you really need in order to sew most garments. To add to your supplies, visit the notions section of your local fabric store or sign up to receive catalogs from sewing-related Web sites.

Basic Tools

Sewing tools have come a long way since the first caveperson sewed two skins together with a "needle" fashioned from a bone! Don't be overwhelmed with the almost infinite choices that are available to you. The basic tools—introduced in this section—still work just fine.

Sewing Machine

You can construct all the garments in this book by hand sewing. However, using a sewing machine is much quicker and easier, and it gives more professional-looking results. There are many different kinds of sewing machines on the market, new and used, from very simple to very complex. Many of the newer, more expensive machines are computerized.

If you plan to purchase a basic sewing machine to sew garments at home, look for one that has the following features.

EASY-FILL BOBBIN CASING

Sewing machines have a bobbin casing into which the bobbin is inserted. While the casing is usually in the same general location on most machines—under where the needle goes up and down through a little hole—how you insert the bobbin in the casing can vary.

Find a machine whose casing is easily accessible. Some machines require you to remove the extension table in order to get to the bobbin, which can make changing the bobbin thread very frustrating.

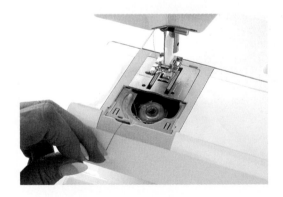

SEVERAL MACHINE STITCHES

Older sewing machines had only the straight stitch. These were followed by machines with the straight stitch and the zigzag stitch. Today's sewing machines often offer a variety of stitches (such as these shown at right) that enable you to add decoration to garments if you choose to do so.

A VARIETY OF MACHINE FEET

Older sewing machines had one presser foot, a zipper foot, and possibly a buttonhole attachment. When zigzag stitches came in, so did the zigzag foot. Today, sewing machine manufacturers typically include a variety of machine feet with the purchase of a machine. You can buy additional specialty sewing machine feet, such as these shown in the photo at right, from your dealer or from sewing supply catalogs.

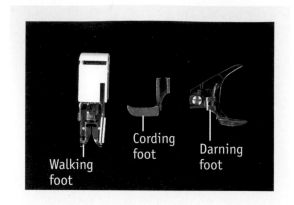

Walking foot

Cording foot

Darning foot

AUTOMATIC BUTTONHOLE ATTACHMENT

Some sewing machines do not have a built-in automatic buttonhole maker or buttonhole attachment. While you can make buttonholes manually with the zigzag stitch, using a buttonhole attachment or a built-in automatic buttonhole stitch is much easier, neater, and more accurate.

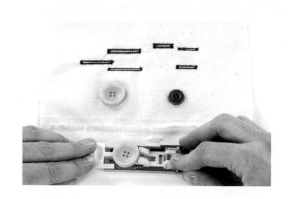

NEEDLE POSITION BUTTON

Older sewing machines did not have a needle up or down stop position button. If you did not check to make sure the needle was in the top position when you stopped sewing and clipped your threads, the thread would be too short and get pulled out of the needle every time you started to sew again.

The needle stop position button enables you to stop the needle in either the top or the bottom position. When the needle stops in the top (up) position, the thread doesn't pull out of the needle when the machine starts again.

By stopping the needle in the bottom (down) position, the needle stays in the fabric, making it easy to turn corners (see Chapter 2).

TIP

Another useful feature is the capability to move the needle from its center position to either the right or the left. This makes under-stitching, topstitching, stitching in the ditch, and using the zipper foot much easier. (See Chapter 2 for more information on these stitches.)

Cutting Tools

SHEARS AND SCISSORS

Purchase a pair of bent-handled shears. The bent angle of the lower blade allows the fabric to remain flat as you cut. The grip should feel comfortable in your hand. Keep these scissors sharp, and do not use them for cutting anything other than fabric.

A small pair of scissors is useful for trimming threads. A pair of pinking shears is useful, but not necessary, for finishing edges.

ROTARY CUTTER, CUTTING MAT, AND STRAIGHTEDGE RULER

A rotary cutter and cutting mat are helpful for cutting long, straight edges. Cut by placing a straightedge ruler on top of the fabric and pattern, holding it firmly, and running the rotary cutter along it. A rotary cutter does not work as well on curves and irregular edges. Rotary cutters, cutting mats, and straightedge rulers come in various sizes.

SEAM RIPPER

Everyone needs a seam ripper to undo mistakes easily. Small scissors also work, but with a seam ripper you are less likely to cut the fabric accidently.

Pins and Needles

PINS

Use clean dressmaker pins with sharp points. The weight of the shaft should be appropriate for the weight of the fabric you're pinning. Glass-headed pins are easier to find when you drop them on the rug!

NOTE: Do not leave pins in your fabric when you're finished sewing for the day. It may be days or weeks before you get back to your project, and some pins rust.

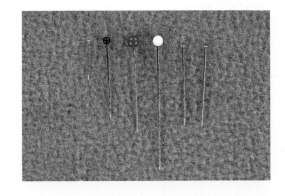

HAND-SEWING NEEDLES

Hand-sewing needles come in a variety of sizes and weights and are designed for a variety of tasks. The key is to keep the needles sharp. If your needles have become dull, throw them out. Dull needles will leave holes in your garments. Have a variety of hand-sewing needles on hand, and select the needle most appropriate to the task, fabric, and thread you are using.

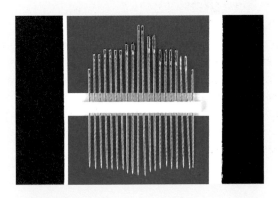

SEWING MACHINE NEEDLES

Sewing machine needles also come in a variety of sizes for different weights and types of fabric. Have a variety of needles on hand, and select the needle most appropriate to the task, fabric, and thread you are using. Look in your sewing machine manual for the correct kind of needle to use for your particular machine.

NOTE: Change your needles often because they can become dull or develop little burrs, which can snag delicate fabrics.

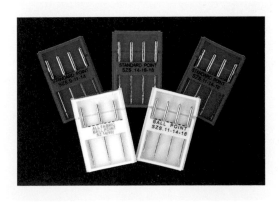

Other Tools

MEASURING TOOLS

A yard/meter stick and a measuring tape are essential measuring tools. A handy addition is a 6-inch sewing gauge. By moving the slider on the sewing gauge, you can easily measure hems, pleats, and other small areas.

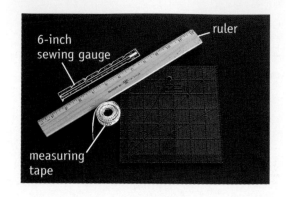

PRESSING TOOLS

All you need for pressing garments are a good steam iron; some type of ironing surface, such as an ironing board; and a supply of pressing cloths. (See "Press Fabric" later in this chapter for more on pressing cloths and how to use them.)

MARKING TOOLS

Marking pens, pencils, tailor's chalk, and dressmaker's carbon and wheels are available in a variety of colors. Most are designed so that their marks disappear with washing. Before using any marking tool, test it on a piece of scrap fabric, just to be sure the marks actually disappear.

Fabric is probably the most fun part of sewing—with the wide array of beautiful options available today, you're sure to build a healthy stash. This section reviews some of the important things to know about choosing, preparing, and caring for fabric.

Terminology

WEAVE

There are two basic "weaves" of fabric: woven and knit. *Woven* fabrics (a), such as wool and cotton, are woven on a loom with a warp and a weft; the warp and weft threads are usually identifiable. *Knits* (b) are just that: knitted, like a sweater. Knits stretch in many directions.

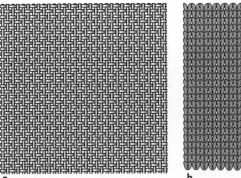
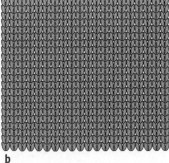

a   b

SELVAGE

The *selvages* are the two finished edges that run the length of the fabric. Some fabrics have a design that runs along one selvage edge. This is often called a *border print fabric*. In this case, extra fabric may be required depending on how you lay the pattern pieces on the fabric. In order to take advantage of the border pattern, several pieces may have to go on the crosswise grain, down the selvage.

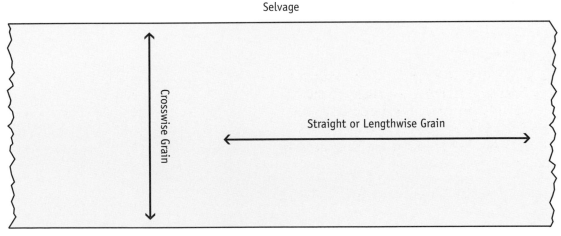

Selvage

Crosswise Grain

Straight or Lengthwise Grain

Selvage

GRAIN

The *straight grain* (or *lengthwise grain*) runs parallel to the selvage. If you pull on the lengthwise grain, there is little, if any, give or stretch. The *crosswise grain* is perpendicular to the selvage. Many fabrics have more stretch on the crosswise grain than the lengthwise grain. Knits and nonwoven fabrics do not have grain.

NOTE: Don't let the terminology confuse you. Sewers often use a variety of words for the same thing. The *straight grain* or *lengthwise grain* can also be called the *longwise grain* or the *straight of grain*.

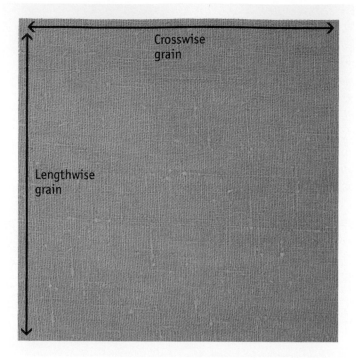

BIAS

The *bias* of fabric runs on the diagonal (45-degree angle) from the selvage. When you pull on the bias, the fabric stretches or gives considerably.

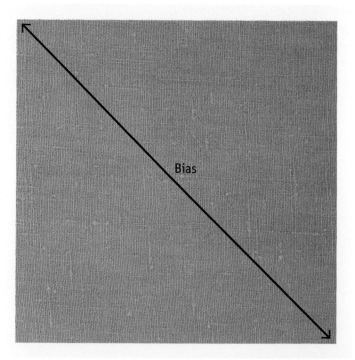

DRAPE

Drape is the quality of fabric that enables it to fall in graceful folds. Take drape into consideration when choosing fabric for a garment. For example, a flowing peasant skirt will not flow or drape well if constructed from heavy, stiff, duck-cloth fabric. Unfold a yard or two of fabric from the bolt, grab a handful, and hold it up, letting it fall naturally over your hand. Does it flow enough or too much for the garment you have in mind?

NAP

Some fabric has a nap caused by the pile. *Pile* is a raised surface of yarn loops sheared rather high to make a soft, velvety surface. Velvet, velveteen, and corduroy are examples of fabric with a nap. If you run your hand lengthwise over the fabric, one way will feel smooth and the other way will feel rough, similar to petting a cat.

NOTE: When making garments from fabric that has a nap, make sure the top and bottom of each pattern piece has the nap going the same way. The color shading is different when the nap is going down than it is when the nap is going up.

Other fabrics with a nap have pictures printed on them so it's clear which end is up. In this case, it's sometimes necessary to purchase extra fabric, because you have to lay all the pattern pieces with the tops of the pieces going in the same direction. The back of the pattern envelope will suggest how much extra fabric you will need.

SIDES

Right, outside, and *public* all refer to the side of the fabric that people looking at you can see. *Wrong* or *inside* refers to the side of the fabric closest to your skin and not seen by those looking at you.

On some fabrics, it is obvious which side is which, and on others, it doesn't matter—both sides are exactly the same. On still others, you have to decide which will be the public side.

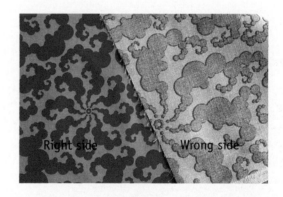

Right side   Wrong side

TIP

Mark the Wrong Side Only

First, decide which side of the fabric is to be seen by the public and which side is not. Put a W on the wrong side of the fabric with a marking pen in the seam allowances. A little piece of masking tape with a *W* for wrong side printed on it also works well.

Prepare Fabric

Before you cut out a pattern, you must prepare the fabric in exactly the same way that you will care for the garment after you make it. If you will wash the garment by hand, wash the fabric by hand. If you plan to wash your garment in the washing machine with detergent, prepare your fabric the same way. (See "Fabric Types and Their Care," later in this chapter.) Certain fabrics, such as wools, may need to be dry cleaned or steamed prior to cutting.

Preparing fabric usually means preshrinking, especially if the fabric is cotton or a cotton blend. You don't want the fabric to shrink after you have made the garment, so shrink it first.

Also, some dyes, especially reds and blues, have a tendency to run. Wash darks and lights in different loads. If you must wash them in the same load after the garment is made, wash your fabric several times before you cut out the pattern, so you don't end up with a totally pink or blue wardrobe.

Fabric Types and Their Care

Some of the most common fabrics used in fashion construction are listed in the table that follows (see pages 16 and 17). If your fabric isn't listed, remember that care instructions can be found on the end of the bolt.

NOTE: When using two different kinds of fabrics in one garment, treat the finished product with the care directions of the more delicate fabric.

Fabric *(continued)*

Fabric	Description	Uses	Washing Care	Pressing Care
Cotton				
Brushed cotton	Warm cotton brushed on one side	Casual shirts, linings, children's wear	Medium	Hot on the wrong side
Chambray	Lightweight, easy to sew plain	Shirts, children's wear	Medium	Hot
Chintz	Closely woven with a glazed finish	Home furnishings, dresses	Dry clean	Medium, wrong side
Corduroy	Lengthwise wale with nap	Skirts, pants, jackets	Cool	Press on top of a towel
Crinkle cotton	Soft, absorbent, and easy to wear	Dresses, blouses	Medium	On the wrong side with a pressing cloth
Denim	Strong, densely woven, twill weave	Jeans, jackets, shirts	Cool	Press while damp
Gingham	Lightweight and strong, small checks white/color	Blouses, skirts, children's wear	Medium	Hot
Jersey	Finely knit, nice drape, crease resistant	Sportswear, T-shirts, dresses	Cool	Use a damp cloth
Lawn	Lightweight, crisp, smooth, absorbent	Blouses, baby dresses	Cool	Gently with slightly warm iron
Muslin	Plain open weave	Test garments	Cool	Use steam
Poplin	Medium weight, cross-rib, absorbent	Shirts, blouses, dresses	Medium	Use a pressing cloth
Seersucker	Lightweight, puckered/flat stripes	Shirts, suits, children's wear	Medium-hot	Don't press unless you really have to
Terrycloth	Uncut loops on one or both sides	Bathrobes	Medium-hot	Too much pressing squashes the fluffiness of terrycloth
Velvet	Silky pile nap on right side	Evening	Dry clean	Press on a needle board
Wool				
Crepe	Fine, soft, textured, nice drape	Dresses, suits	Dry clean	Press on the wrong side
Challis	Lightweight, soft, nice drape, often with an overall pattern	Dresses, skirts	Hand	Use a damp cloth
Flannel	Strong, nap on one or both sides	Suits, jackets, shirts, pants	Hand wash or dry clean	Press on the wrong side
Gabardine	Wool blend with close twill weave	Pants	Dry clean	Press on the wrong side; use a damp cloth
Jersey, single	Knit, vertical ribs on right side	Casual, children's wear, athletic apparel	Cool	Use a damp cloth
Jersey, double	Knit, vertical ribs on both sides, firmer than single	Suits	Cool	Use a damp cloth
Worsted	Tightly woven, hard wearing	Suits, coats	Dry clean	Use a damp cloth

Linen

Handkerchief	Fine, sheer, lightweight, nice drape, soft crispness	Blouses	Cool	Press on the wrong side; use a damp cloth
Linen/silk	Soft crispness, often striped	Suits, skirts, dresses, pants	Dry clean	Press on the wrong side
Suiting	Crisp, strong, absorbent, wrinkles easily	Shirts, skirts, jackets	Dry clean	Press on the wrong side while damp

Silk

Chiffon	Open weave, sheer, nice drape	Evening, blouses	Cool	Do not use steam
Georgette	Loose weave, sheer	Blouses, dresses, evening	Dry clean	Do not use steam
Organza	Very fine weave, transparent, stiff	Trim, collars, facings, bridal	Dry clean	Gently with slightly warm iron
Shantung	Medium weight with a rough texture	Shirts, dresses, pants	Dry clean	Do not use steam
Silk satin	Smooth, lustrous finish on one side	Dresses, jackets, evening	Dry clean	Do not use steam
Taffeta	Smooth, crisp, lustrous finish	Dresses, jackets, bridal, evening	Dry clean	Do not use steam

Synthetic

Acetate	Lustrous, nice drape	Dresses, athletic apparel	Dry clean	Press on the wrong side, do not use steam
Acrylic	Lightweight knit	Sports	Cool	Cool iron
Bouclé	Loosely woven or knitted; loopy threads look bulky	Suits	Cool	Press on the wrong side; use a damp cloth
Charmeuse	Fine satin with shiny right side and a matte back side	Blouses	Cool	Press on the wrong side
Georgette	Sheer	Blouses, dresses, evening	Dry clean	Do not use steam
Lamé	Knit or woven, smooth, shiny made with metallic yarns	Evening	Dry clean	Use a dry iron and a pressing cloth
Nylon	Strong, lightweight, nonabsorbent	Rain gear, ski clothing	Cool	Cool iron
Polar fleece	Soft, lightweight with a brushed surface	Outdoor	Cool	Little need to iron
Polyester crepe	Soft, crease resistant, nice drape, wears well	Blouses, dresses, evening	Cool	Slightly warm iron
Polyester/ linen	Looks like linen but doesn't wrinkle	Suits, dresses	Cool	Slightly warm iron
Rayon	From plant cellulose, absorbent	Many uses	Read label	Read the label
Spandex	Lightweight, stretchy	Casual, athletic apparel	Cool	Do not press
Tulle	Small mesh net made from nylon	Petticoats, bridal, costumes	Hand wash cool	Usually not pressed as it would lose its stiffness
Viscose	Soft, absorbent, nice drape, made from wood pulp or cotton waste	Dresses, skirts	Cool, dry clean	Press on the wrong side

Press Fabric

Pressing is slightly different than ironing. When ironing, you push the iron back and forth over the garment. When pressing, there is almost no back-and-forth motion. You put the iron down on the garment and lift it up. Then you put it down in another location and lift it up again.

 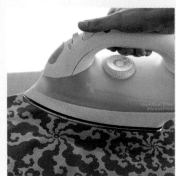

Down   *Up*

Some fabrics should be pressed only on the wrong side so that you don't create a "shine" on the fabric. Some need to be pressed with a pressing cloth. You can purchase pressing cloths or use a clean, soft piece of white or neutral fabric (cotton, muslin, or linen). An old, clean linen handkerchief also works well. If you purchase new fabric for pressing, wash it several times to get the sizing off.

A pressing cloth can be used either dry or damp. To use a damp pressing cloth, soak it in water and thoroughly wring it out. Place the damp cloth on the item to be pressed, and, with the steam on the iron turned off, put the iron on the pressing cloth. Pick up and move the pressing cloth around as needed, but do not move the garment being pressed around until it's thoroughly dry; in its dampened state, it is easily pulled out of shape.

Thread

Since embroidery machines entered the home sewing market, hundreds of new types of thread have appeared. Different threads vary in fiber content, fiber length, thread size, and intended use. Remember that your project will look and stand up better if you use a high-quality thread instead of a cheap thread.

For most home fashion sewing, you should use an all-purpose thread. Another option is to use cotton thread on cotton fabric, silk thread on silk fabric, and so on. Pick a color that matches the fabric. If you can't find an exact match, find the next darker shade, because thread tends to sew in one shade lighter.

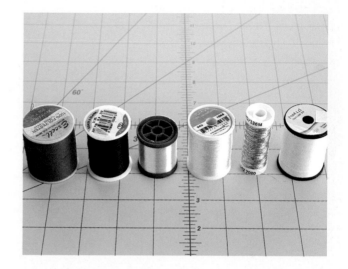

① Polyester cotton is an all-purpose thread. It is strong and has some elasticity.

② Cotton thread is used for hand and machine stitching.

③ Invisible thread is used when you don't want the thread to show. Be careful when pressing garments sewn with invisible thread; the thread might melt!

④ Silk thread is very strong and works best on wool and silk fabrics.

⑤ Metallic thread, usually silver or gold, is used when you want fancy decorative stitches. Metallic thread tends to be heat sensitive, so press carefully.

⑥ Button thread for sewing on buttons is extra strong and extra thick. Do not use it on delicate fabrics.

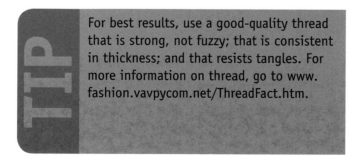

TIP

For best results, use a good-quality thread that is strong, not fuzzy; that is consistent in thickness; and that resists tangles. For more information on thread, go to www.fashion.vavpycom.net/ThreadFact.htm.

CHAPTER 2

Technique Review

Now that you have gathered most of your supplies, let's review some of the techniques you need to know to make the garments in this book. If you are new to sewing, take some time to practice some of these techniques on scraps of fabric.

This chapter is a review of the basics, not a compendium of every sewing skill there is. As with most things, there are many different ways to accomplish the same task. I demonstrate several methods for some tasks, but you don't need to be an expert in all the variations. Try out the different methods, find the one that works for you, and stick with it.

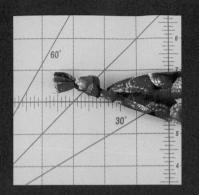

Basic Machine Stitches

To complete the garments in this book and to be able to use almost any sewing pattern on the market, you need only the following machine stitches. Don't be overwhelmed by all the suggested possibilities in your sewing machine manual or by some complicated-looking garment.

STRAIGHT SEAM

Whether you are stitching by hand or on a sewing machine, the process of sewing two or more separate pieces of fabric together is referred to as "sewing a seam." The basic *straight seam* (because of its straight stitches) is the most common stitch used to construct a garment and the simplest to master.

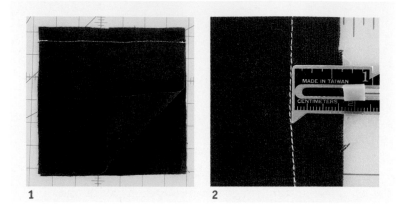

1

2

1. Put the right sides of the fabric pieces together with the raw edges even.

2. Using a ⅝-inch seam allowance or the seam allowance suggested by the pattern, stitch the seam.

3. Back-tack (also called *backstitch*) at each end of the seam to secure the stitching. Your sewing machine should have a backstitch button that you can push for the machine to stitch backward. When you come to the end of the seam, push the backstitch button and stitch back over the previous stitching for about an inch.

4. Press the seam open.

3

TOPSTITCH

Topstitching shows on the outside of a garment and is occasionally functional (as in a plain straight stitch), but more often a fancy decorative stitch. Use a thread color that matches or contrasts with the fabric you've chosen.

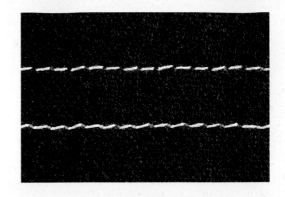

Work from the right side of the fabric. Sew a line of stitches ¼ inch from the edge and parallel to the edge. The edge can also be a seam line, as decorative top-stitching on a collar, lapel, or cuff.

The pattern will indicate how many rows and the location of the topstitching, or you can do your own thing to get the look that you want by using a decorative stitch and contrasting thread as shown in the photo.

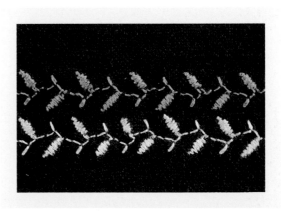

UNDERSTITCH

Understitching is a line of stitching through the facing and seam allowances used to keep collars, cuffs, armholes or front facings, and waistbandless waist edges from rolling and exposing the lining, under collar, cuff, or facing to the public.

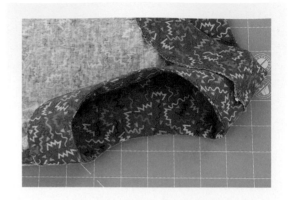

❶ After you have sewn the seam to attach a facing or lining, turn the garment to the inside.

❷ Press both the seam allowances toward the lining/facing side and away from the garment.

2

❸ From the right side of the facing/lining, sew the facing/lining and seam allowances together about ⅛ inch away from the seam line. Be careful not to sew in the seam line.

3

STITCH IN THE DITCH

Stitching in the ditch means stitching directly over stitches in a seam. Stitching in the ditch is very popular with quilters. In garment sewing, it is used primarily for attaching the backside (inside) of a waistband without hand sewing.

1. Before sewing the waistband to the garment, fold the inside bottom edge of the waistband toward the wrong side and press on the seam line.

2. Sew the right side of the waistband to the right side of the garment at the waistline, press the waistband up, and fold over so that the folded line made in Step 1 just covers the seam line you just made.

3. From the right side of the garment, pin the back of the waistband down by placing the pins in the seam line (Step 2). Be careful to catch the inside of the waistband with the pins. The heads of the pins should be toward you and the points should be away from you when the garment is placed on the sewing machine and the waistband is to the right.

1

3

4. Pulling the seam as flat as possible, stitch in the seam over your previous stitching, pulling the pins out as you go.

See Chapter 6 for more details of stitching in the ditch.

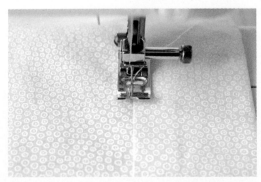

4

Useful Hand Stitches

Today, most hand stitches are used for basting and finishing. Use hand stitching for stitching that is going to be removed and not seen on soft or filmy fabrics. It's easier to pull out hand basting than it is to pull out machine basting, and sometimes the holes made from the machine basting show. It's also easier to put in hand basting in small places, such as collars. (See Chapter 5 for more hand stitches.)

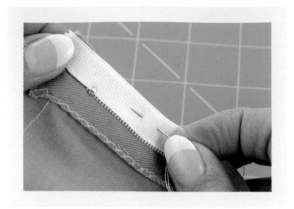

RUNNING STITCH

The running stitch is used mostly for basting and gathering if the stitches are long and for simple seams if the stitches are short.

① Work from right to left. Pick up several stitches on the needle by inserting the needle from the top, picking up some fabric from below, and reinserting the needle from below.

② When the needle is full of stitches, slowly pull the thread through all the stitches.

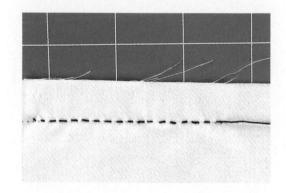

There are at least three ways to deal with the end of the thread so it doesn't pull through when you start to gather:

- Leave a long tail and hold the tail between your fingers as you gather.

- Tie a knot at one end and gather from the other end, as in the photo.

- Put a pin perpendicular to the edge at the beginning of the section to be gathered, and wrap the thread around the pin several times in a crossover pattern.

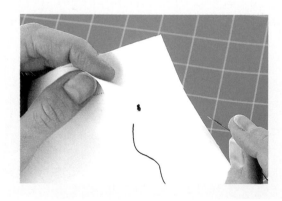

SLIP STITCH

The slip stitch is usually used to sew two folded edges together in such a way that the stitches do not show. It is useful for tacking facings down to seam allowances or for stitching together the top of a slit where the machine stitches have come undone. Make the stitches small and invisible.

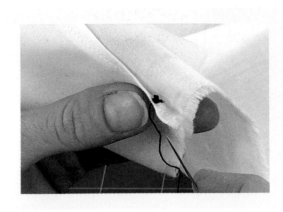

1 Work from right to left. Make a small stitch, less than ¼ inch, right in the fold of one of the pieces being sewn together using matching thread. Contrasting thread was used in the photo for better visibility.

2 Where the needle comes out of the first fold, insert the needle into the other fold. Repeat back and forth, keeping the thread hidden in the folds.

3 When sewing a folded edge to another fabric, bring the needle out through the folded edge.

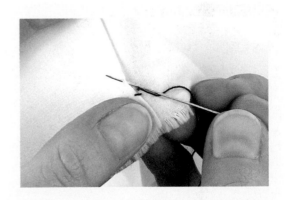

4 Pick up a thread from the second fabric and insert the needle back into the folded edge in the same location. Try to have as little thread show as possible.

NOTE: The example here shows contrasting thread so that you can see how seams are made. In actual garments, you would use coordinating thread.

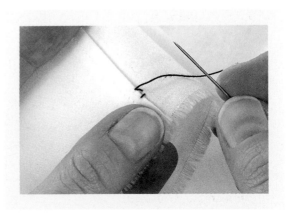

Tacks

There are two commonly used basic techniques in sewing that are referred to as *tacks*. *Tailor tacks* are used to transfer the location of pattern dots from the pattern to the fabric. (See Chapter 3 for more on pattern dots and notches.) *Thread chain tacks* are used to hold a lining to a skirt or as buttonholes.

Tailor Tacks

Use tailor tacks on fabric that's difficult to mark with a marking pen or pencil or with carbon paper, such as wool. Tailor tacks are made with the pattern still pinned to the fabric. Put a tailor tack on every dot you see on the pattern. Use a long double thread without a knot at the end.

① Take a stitch through the pattern and all layers of fabric. Put the needle in at 3 o'clock on the marked dot, and bring it out at 9 o'clock. Leave a long tail of thread.

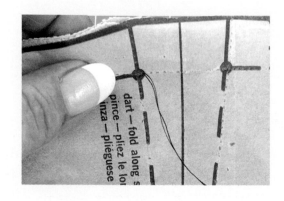

② Repeat by putting the needle in the dot at 6 o'clock and bringing it out at 12 o'clock. Don't pull the stitch down tight; leave a large loop. Cut the thread, leaving another long tail of thread. Make a tailor tack on all the dots and markings on all the pattern pieces.

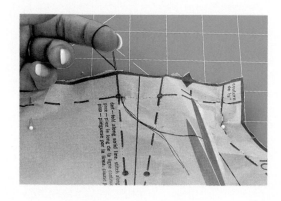

③ When you're ready to sew a particular pattern piece, cut the loops at the top. Carefully pull the pattern pieces from the fabric.

NOTE: Do not cut the loops on all the pattern pieces at once because they may come undone before you're ready to sew that piece.

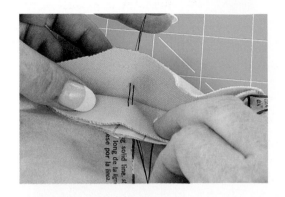

④ Lift one of the fabric pieces slightly and snip the threads between the pieces. Be careful not to pull the thread out of the top fabric. You can prevent this by making the tails and loops long enough.

See Chapter 3 for more information on tailor tacks.

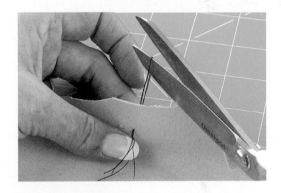

TIP

Remember to pull the tailor tack threads after you have sewn the garment together. If you have sewn over them, pull the threads carefully so as not to undo the stitching of the seam.

Tacks *(continued)*

Thread Chain Tacks

To keep a lining in place or to prevent it from twisting, use a thread chain tack near the hemline.

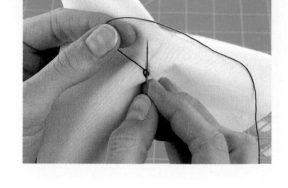

1 Thread a hand-sewing needle with a double thread and knot the threads together. Attach the thread securely to the inside of a seam about 2 inches up from the bottom of the garment or near the top of the hem. Do not let your stitches show on the outside of the garment. To make a stitch, wrap the thread around the double strand of thread secured in the seam, leaving a long loop.

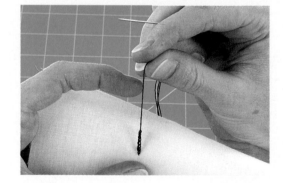

2 Insert two fingers into the loop, catch the needle and thread being held in the other hand, and pull it through the loop. Tighten the first loop by pulling it snug and sliding it up to the top where the double strand was secured in the seam. Continue making wrapped stitches and sliding them snugly up against the previous loop.

NOTE: If you know how to crochet a chain stitch, the process is the same, only you use your fingers in place of the crochet hook.

3 Continue making the chain for about 1 inch. Secure the chain to the seam allowance of the lining by taking a stitch in the lining seam allowance.

You can use a similar method to make a thread chain to form a small button loop for a ball button at the top of a back neck closure on a blouse. (See the reference later in this chapter under "Thread Chain.")

Finish a seam to make the inside of your garment look tidy and to keep the raw edges of the seam allowances from fraying. Do the edge finishes before constructing the garment. This will keep the edges from raveling or keep the shape of something—such as a curved neckline—from being stretched and distorted during the handling and construction process.

PINKED

The easiest way to create an edge finish is to use your pinking shears, if you have them, and trim all the seam allowances. This method works best on tightly woven fabrics that have a minimum amount of fray.

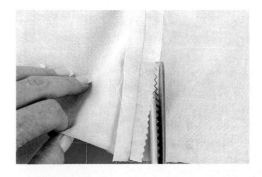

STAY-STITCHED

Stay-stitching is the most commonly used edge finish on woven fabrics. If the fabric has a tendency to fray, first sew a straight line of stitching ¼ inch from the edge on all seam allowances whether pinked or straight-cut.

TIP

There are several methods for finishing seams; keep the kind of fabric in mind when deciding which method to use. For example, French seams are better for slippery, sheer fabrics. The single-fold seam finish does not work as well for heavy wools because of the bulk.

ZIGZAG

If the fabric is relatively firm, zigzag all the edges. If the fabric is softer, zigzag at least ¼ inch in from the edge.

SINGLE FOLD

If the fabric is closely woven and not too bulky, after a straight seam has been sewn, you can fold the raw edge ¼ inch to the wrong side, press, and stitch the "hem" close to the fold line.

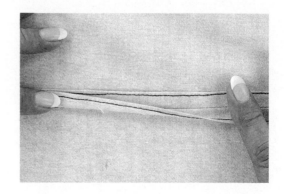

FRENCH SEAMS

On see-through fabrics, use French seams. This is a kind of seam in which the raw edges of the seam are encased by a second seam on the inside of the garment; thus, the inside seam allowances that are visible from the public side look neater. French seams used to be a mark of quality and indicated a better-made garment.

NOTE: The example here shows contrasting thread so that you can see how seams are made. In actual garments, you would sew in coordinating thread.

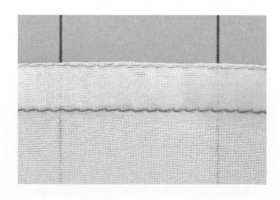

① With wrong sides together, sew a ¼-inch seam.

② Press the seam to one side.

③ Turn the fabric so that the right sides are together, and press the seam.

④ With right sides together, sew a ⅜-inch seam. The seam allowance will be encased in the new seam.

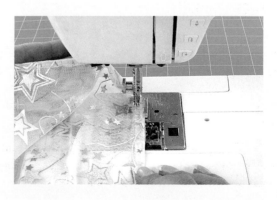

Straps, Ties, and Belts

There are two basic methods of making straps, ties, and belts. Even if a pattern suggests one method, you're free to choose the method that works best for you. The fabric you choose will also help you decide. Making a very narrow strap from wool with the sew-and-turn method (Method 1) or making a very narrow strap from a slippery, filmy fabric with the press-and-sew method (Method 2) requires patience and practice. For very long ties, the press-and-sew method works better.

Method 1: Sew and Turn

This method is used on lighter-weight fabrics such as the straps on a sundress.

1. Fold the strip in half lengthwise with right sides together. Do not press.

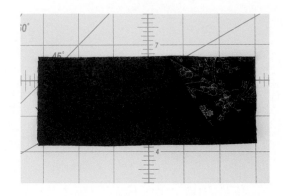

2. Pin the edges together.

 Most straps, ties, and belts are cut on the straight grain unless otherwise indicated on the pattern. If you cut off-grain, the strap, tie, or belt tends to twist and not lie flat.

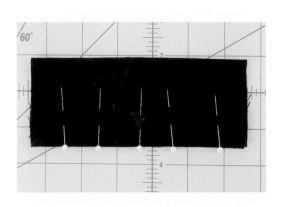

③ Begin in the center of the open edge and stitch to the end, leaving the needle down. If you need to finish one of the short sides of the piece, turn the corner, and finish the end.

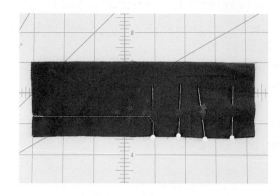

④ Leave about a 2-inch opening for turning the strap or tie right side out after you've finished stitching to the other end. If you need to finish one of the short sides of the piece, turn the corner and finish the end.

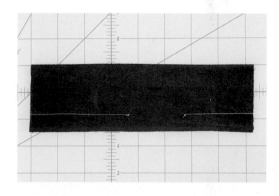

⑤ Use a safety pin or a turning tool to turn the strip right side out and push the corners out.

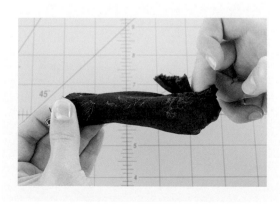

6 Press flat with the seam on one edge.

The finished strap or tie is ready to be sewn to the garment.

NOTE: If you don't want the seam on the edge, leave the ends open in steps 3 and 4. Turn the strip right side out, and press flat so that the seam runs down the middle of one side. Finish the ends.

TIP

There are several different ways to finish the ends of straps, ties, and belts. How you finish the ends depends on taste, purpose, and design. You can tie an overhand knot, fray the ends, add trim, or tuck the ends to the inside and topstitch closed. For more detail, see the "Finish the Ends" section, later in this chapter.

Method 2: Press and Sew

Try this method if the weight of the fabric is heavy and the strap is narrow.

1 Press the seam allowance on both long edges to the inside (wrong side).

2 Press the fabric in half lengthwise with the wrong sides together.

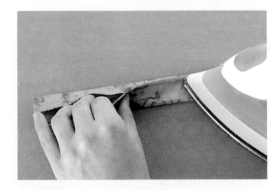

3 Begin in the middle of the strip, and, going to both ends, pin the folded edges together in several places.

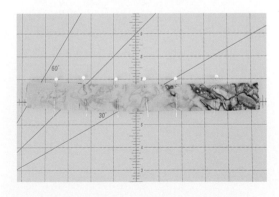

④ Tuck the seam allowance on both ends of the strip to the inside, pin, and press the ends.

⑤ Topstitch the strap together close to the edge.

TIP

If your strap is more than 1 inch wide and you want to give the strap some body so that it won't crinkle or roll up, put a piece of fusible interfacing on the inside of the strap. The interfacing should be half the width and the whole length of the strap.

To make spaghetti straps stronger, do not trim the seam allowances too close to the seam line.

Finish the Ends

STRAPS FOR DRESSES AND TOPS

While straps, belts, and ties are all made in basically the same way, straps are typically attached to a garment at one or both ends. As with most sewing techniques, you have a variety of options to choose from.

Most straps for dresses and tops are sewn to the inside of the bodice. The ends of these straps do not need to be finished. The raw edges will be hidden inside the garment.

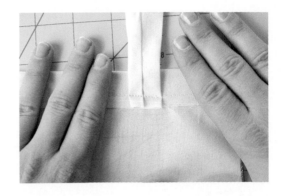

OVER-THE-SHOULDER STRAPS THAT FASTEN

For over-the-shoulder straps that fasten in the front with a button or snap, leave the end that is sewn into the back of the bodice open. Finish the end that has the fastener. The end can be square, round, or diagonal. Before sewing the length together, draw the shape you want on one end of the strap. Don't forget to allow for seam allowances. When sewing the length together, finish the end by sewing on the line you have drawn. Trim the sewn end before you turn the strap right side out.

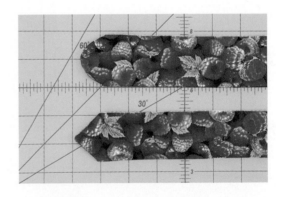

TIED AND FRAYED ENDS

Tie ends can be left unfinished and tied with a simple overhand half-knot. Also, some fabrics fray nicely on ties and belts. It must be a straight edge and not a curved edge. Sew a line of stitching across the belt or tie with either straight or decorative stitches at least 1 inch from the ends. Fringe the frayed ends by gently pulling out the threads back to the stitching.

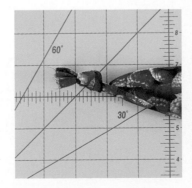
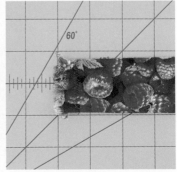

Closures

There are many different types of closures. Your pattern will make a suggestion, but which one you choose is up to you. When deciding which closure to use, take into consideration how much wear and tear the closure is going to have to withstand, what closure is best for your fabric and garment design, and whether the closure is going to be seen as part of your garment or be invisible.

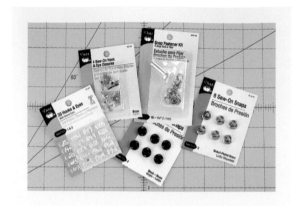

Ties and Buttons

TIES

Ties are used for closures on wraparound skirts, straps on sundresses, and some wraparound blouses. Make ties from matching or contrasting fabric. (For more on ties, see the "Straps, Ties, and Belts" section, earlier in this chapter.)

BUTTONS

The sizes, colors, and shapes of buttons available to home sewers today are almost endless. Buttons can be functional or decorative or both. There are two basic button designs: those with holes and those with shanks. Buttons with holes have either two or four holes, while shank buttons have raised shanks with holes in the shanks on the bottoms of the buttons.

When sewing on a button, use double thread, but knot each strand separately. Doing so prevents the thread from getting tangled. Beginning on the underside of the fabric, stick the needle up through the fabric and through one of the button's holes. Put the needle back through a different hole. Continue until the button is secure.

BUTTONHOLES

There are a variety of ways to make buttonholes. The easiest is with a buttonhole attachment that comes with most sewing machines or a built-in automatic buttonhole stitch. Your pattern directions will suggest what size buttons to use and show you where to place the button-holes and buttons.

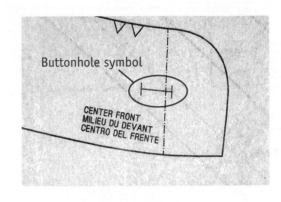

THREAD CHAIN

Thread chains can be used in place of buttonholes at back necklines, when the button is small, functional, and minimally decorative. Out of thread, make the chain length just long enough to go over the button (for instructions, see the "Thread Chain Tacks" section, ear-lier in this chapter). Secure the thread in the facing seam at the top of the back neck slit, securing the bot-tom of the loop about ¼ inch to ⅜ inch lower. This will be a small loop; you won't be able to get two fingers inside it. Use thread the same color as the garment (the photo uses contrasting thread for better visibility).

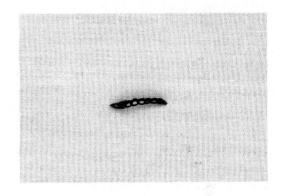

FABRIC AND ELASTIC LOOPS

Following the press-and-sew method for making straps (see page 37), make a strap about ⅜ inch wide. Cut the strip into lengths long enough to loop over your but-tons, and stitch in the seam between the facing and the garment.

For many small buttons close together, as on the back of a wedding dress or on a skirt, buy a tape of elastic but-ton loops (shown here) instead of making dozens of individual buttonhole loops. Sew the tape on the inside of the garment with the loops extended and available to loop around the buttons.

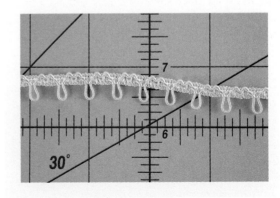

Snaps, Hooks, and Eyes

Snaps work well on lightweight fabrics where the closures don't get much wear and tear. They come in various diameters and weights and are usually black, silver, or white.

Caution: Small snaps do not work well on the waists of skirts. Snaps, in general, do not work on blouse fronts at the point of the bust line; they pop open too easily. Snaps do help as a secondary defense along with a button or hook and eye.

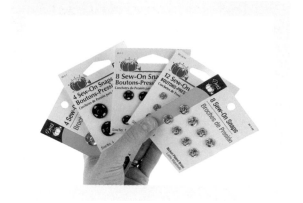

SEW ON SNAPS

1 On the wrong side of the overlapping edge, sew the snap half with the ball. Sew several stitches through each hole on the snap, being careful not to have the stitches show on the right side of the garment.

2 Use tailor's chalk to coat the ball of the snap. Bring the fabric that will be holding the other half of the snap over so that the ball of the snap marks on the fabric. This shows you where to sew the other half of the snap.

3 Center the snap half with the socket over the mark, and sew several stitches through each hole on the snap.

2

NONSEW SNAPS

There are also nonsew snaps. Attaching them requires a special tool (shown here). These tools are readily available wherever nonsew snaps are sold. Just follow the directions on the package.

You can also purchase snap tape by the yard. The snaps are attached to a tape. Snap tape is especially good on the inseam of toddler pants. After the garment is finished, stitch one half of the tape to one side of the inseam opening and the other half to the other side of the opening. Be sure to line up the snaps on both sides so they will snap together.

HOOKS AND EYES

There are several variations on the hook and eye. Some have looped eyes, and some have straight eyes. They are often used on waistbands, at the top of a zipper, or at the back neck edge of a top or dress. They are usually silver, black, or white and come in various sizes. Choose the weight and size to match your fabric weight and function.

1 Sew the eyes onto the right side of the underlap. You don't need to break the thread after sewing through the first hole. Slide the needle between the layers of fabric and continue sewing the second hole.

2 Position the hook part close to the edge on the underside of the overlap and sew several stitches in each hole of the hook, making sure the hooks and eyes match up with the right amount of overlap. Be sure none of your stitches show on the right side of the overlap.

HOOK-AND-LOOP TAPE

Hook-and-loop fastener tape has become very popular in the last decade. It comes in a variety of colors and can be purchased by the yard or in various sizes of dots, squares, and rectangles. Some tapes come with a sticky adhesive backing, and others need to be sewn on by hand or by machine.

NOTE: Do not sew the kind of hook-and-loop tape with a self-adhesive backing by hand or on your machine. The adhesive really clogs your needle.

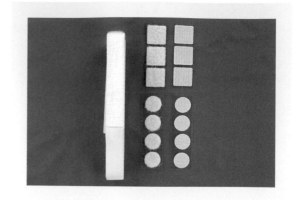

Zippers

Zippers are a relatively recent innovation in the fashion industry. Until the mid-1900s, closures on clothing were accomplished by buttons, ties, snaps, and hooks and eyes. Zippers are available in several different weights, lengths, and colors to match your fabric. Home sewers have their own favorite ways to put in zippers. Most zippers come in a package that includes instructions for sewing in a zipper.

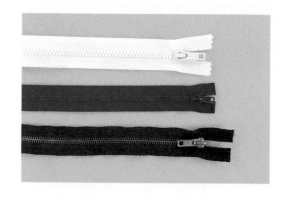

There are two kinds of zippers: regular and invisible. The differences between the two are apparent when they are sewn into the garments, as well as in the final look. For example, when putting a regular zipper in a back seam, you sew the seam first and then sew in the zipper. When putting in an invisible zipper, you sew the zipper in first, and then you finish the seam. The difference in the final look is that with a regular zipper the stitching shows on the right side, and with an invisible zipper no stitching is visible on the outside.

CENTERED REGULAR ZIPPERS

Centered regular zippers are easy to sew in. They're often found in the back seams of skirts and dresses. The package that comes with the zipper suggests a method for inserting the zipper. Your sewing machine manual and commercial pattern also will have directions. You will need the zipper foot that came with your machine.

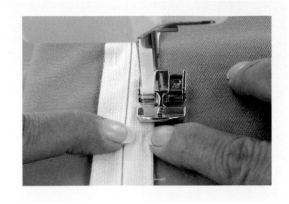

Here's another method:

① Mark on the seam allowance where the bottom of the zipper will be. This is the length of the zipper plus 1 inch. Sew the normal seam to the mark, then backstitch and change to a machine-basting stitch. Machine baste the seam where the zipper will be placed.

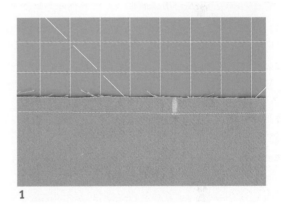

1

② Finish the seams, if desired, and then press the seam flat. Then press the seam from the right side of the fabric.

③ Open (unzip) the zipper. From the wrong side and starting from the top edge, pin one side of the open zipper to the seam allowance, aligning the zipper teeth with the seam line.

④ Hand baste the side of the zipper you have just pinned (see photo). Close the zipper. Hand baste the opposite side to the other seam allowance, keeping the teeth aligned over the seam.

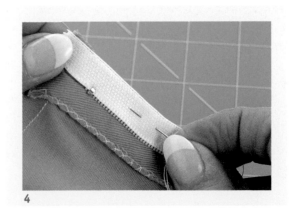

4

5 With the zipper hand-basted in place, remove the pins. Attach the zipper foot to your sewing machine, and align the zipper foot edge with the machine needle.

Stitch down the center of the zipper tape through the seam allowance and garment.

6 Continue sewing to the end of the zipper teeth. Pivot the needle at the base of the zipper teeth, and sew horizontally across the bottom of the zipper. Pivot again in the middle of the tape on other side of the zipper and sew as you did the previous side.

NOTE: Go slowly when you're sewing zippers, and don't be afraid to rip out and redo work if the zipper or fabric turns out puckered or misaligned.

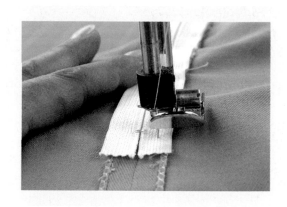

7 When you finish sewing down one side, along the bottom, and up the other side, take the piece out of the machine. Check to be sure the zipper looks neat and aligned.

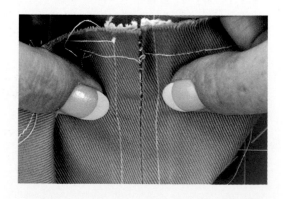

8 If the zipper is neat and properly aligned, use a seam ripper to remove your hand-basting stitches.

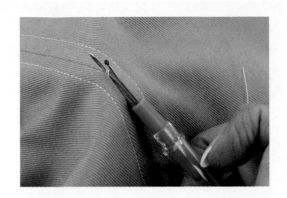

LAPPED REGULAR ZIPPERS

Lapped zippers are usually found in side seams and occasionally in back seams, as on a tailored blouse or dress. A lapped zipper has the zipper hidden behind one fold of fabric. The centered zipper is centered and hidden behind two folds of fabric.

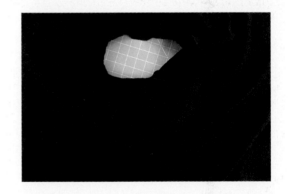

1 Mark on the seam allowance where the bottom of the zipper will be. This is the length of the zipper plus 1 inch. Sew the normal seam to the mark, then backstitch and change to a machine-basting stitch. Machine-baste the seam where the zipper will be placed.

2 Finish the seams, if desired, and then press the seam flat. Then press the seam from the right side of the fabric. Close the zipper, and place it pull-side down on the right side of the seam allowance. Align the zipper teeth to the seam (see photo).

3 Using the zipper foot and starting from the bottom of the zipper, sew the zipper tape to the seam allowance.

4 Flip the zipper so that the pull side is up. Press the seam that is attached to the zipper tape to the seam allowance.

2

5 With the zipper pulled up, sew the pressed edge of the fabric to the zipper tape. (Note that to do this, you'll need to use the opposite side of the zipper foot from the side you used in Step 3.)

5

6 Lay the garment flat and bring the zipper over the right side seam allowance. The seam you sewed in step 5 makes a small pleat (lap).

7 Starting at the bottom, sew the zipper across the zipper teeth, pivot, and sew up the opposite side.

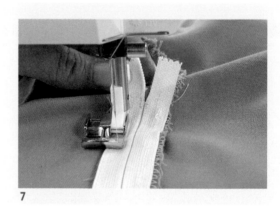

7

8 Check to be sure the zipper looks neat. When you're satisfied with the results, carefully cut the seam basting and press.

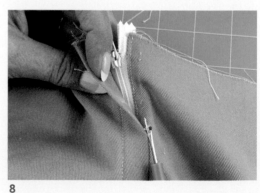

8

TIP

There are many ways to put in lapped zippers. For practice, try a variety of ways until you feel comfortable with one method. Then stick with it. There really is no right or wrong way to put in a zipper. The goal is that the zipper functions and is neatly inserted into the garment.

INVISIBLE ZIPPERS

The teeth of an invisible zipper are hidden in such a way that the seam looks as if it had been sewn together without a zipper or any other type of closure fastening. These zippers work well in any seam and are lightweight, making them a wise choice for evening wear as well as for casual wear. You need a special zipper foot (available in a wide variety of colors!) to insert an invisible zipper. These are readily available wherever invisible zippers are sold. Some sewing machine manufacturers now include this foot with their machines.

1 Unzip the zipper. Using a cool iron, press the zipper coils flat. Keep the zipper and the garment right sides together with the coils along the seam line and the zipper tape in the seam allowance.

NOTE: Unlike the centered and lapped zippers, you do not sew the seam in which an invisible zipper appears until after you sew in the zipper.

2 Position the zipper foot so the needle clears the center hole and the coils glide under the groove; you're stitching on the zipper tape right beside the zipper coils. Sew from the top of the zipper to the bottom of the first piece of fabric. You won't be able to get all the way to the bottom of the zipper.

3 As you sew, be sure that the zipper coil is positioned in the groove of the zipper foot; this will guide the zipper coils.

④ Repeat this stitching on the other side of the zipper and with the other piece of fabric.

You now have the zipper sewn to the two loose pieces of the garment, as in the photo.

⑤ Pull the end of the zipper tape slightly to one side and pin to the seam allowance. Lower the needle just slightly above the end of the zipper stitching and approximately $1/8$ inch to the left of the bottom of the zipper stitching.

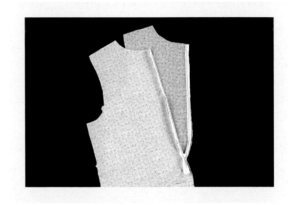

⑥ Lower the zipper foot and sew about 2 inches. This will hold the ends of the zipper together and away from the seam.

⑦ Use a regular machine presser foot and zipper foot to finish sewing the seam. If you desire, finish the raw edges of the seam.

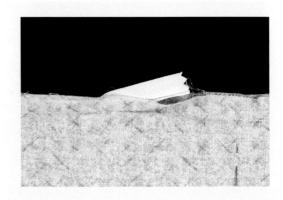

Fashion design is basically taking a flat piece of fabric and shaping it to fit the human body in a pleasing way. The shaping is accomplished with seams, tucks, darts, pleats, gathers, shirring, and smocking.

Types of Shaping

DARTS

Darts are one of the primary methods for shaping a garment. A dart is stitched with a tapering seam. On dresses, darts that cross the waistline are tapered at both ends. One end provides shaping for the bust, while the other end provides fullness for the hips. The widest part of the dart shapes the waist. For more on darts, see chapters 3 and 6.

TIP

Many shaping techniques are interchangeable. For example, if a pattern calls for gathers, you can often change that shaping method to pleats instead. Doing so may also change the style and look of the garment. Pleats tend to give a garment a more formal look than gathers do.

TUCKS

Tucks are stitched folds of the fabric used for shaping. They are similar to darts except the stitching is parallel to the fold.

PLEATS

Pleats are most often used in skirts. The pleats take in fullness at the waist, but, unlike tucks, they are not stitched down, so they allow fullness at the hemline. (For more on pleats, see Chapter 3 and Chapter 6.)

GATHERS

Gathers also take in fullness at the top while allowing fullness at the bottom. Gathers create a more casual look than pleats. (For more on gathers, see Chapter 3 and Chapter 6.)

SHIRRING

Shirring is machine gathers worked in rows. It is usually sewn with a cotton top thread and an elastic bobbin thread, which allows the shirred section to stretch around curves, such as busts and waists. (For specific information on shirring waistlines, see Chapter 6.)

Casings

Acasing is a tunnel of fabric made by two parallel lines of stitching. Cords, ties, or elastic are threaded through the casing. Casings are used on the waists of skirts, pants, and dresses; on necklines; on sleeves; and on pants. Wherever you use a cord, tie, or elastic, you may use a casing. (For information on the use of casing in waistlines, see Chapter 6.)

Types of Casing

SELF

If the edge is cut on the straight or crosswise grain, it's possible to turn over a double-fold hem and stitch the hem down, leaving an opening through which elastic, cords, or ties can be inserted, thereby allowing the tunnel/casing for a cord or elastic to pass through. (See Chapter 6 for more information on self casings.)

BIAS TAPE

If the edge is curved or cut on the bias, it's better to use single-fold bias tape to form the casing. You may want to make your own single-fold bias tape if you can't find the right color or width of purchased bias tape. Usually, the casing doesn't show, depending on where the casing is placed. (See Chapter 6 for more information on making a bias-tape casing.)

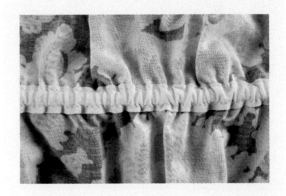

ELASTIC

Elastic is often used inside the casing to provide shaping and stretch. Select the width and type of elastic appropriate for your garment. Cut the length at least 1 inch longer than you need. Thread the elastic through the casing, being careful not to lose the end.

NOTE: One way to keep from losing the end is to pin a large safety pin to the end; the pin needs to be larger than the hole of the casing. Another way is to pin the end of the elastic to the garment in the seam allowance.

Overlap the two ends of the elastic by ½ inch, and stitch securely together with a zigzag stitch. (See Chapter 6 for more information about elastic casing.)

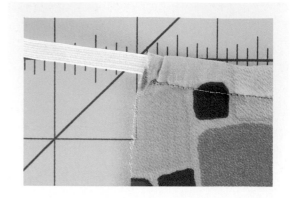

SLITS

Leave an opening in the casing to slip the cord or elastic through. If the opening is going to show (for example, on a pair of pants with a drawstring at the waist), make a buttonhole where you want the ties to emerge from the casing before you sew the casing down. (For more information on casing slits, see Chapter 6.)

TIP

If you're putting elastic in the casing and the casing and the elastic are not going to show, leave an inch unsewn on one side of the casing. After the elastic has been inserted and securely sewn together, finish sewing the casing closed. (For more information on putting elastic in casings, see Chapter 6.)

Points, corners, curves, and graded seams are found mostly on tops with collars, cuffs, and lapels. Points and corners are also found on ties, belts, and straps. To eliminate bulk and to allow fabrics to lie flat, it's necessary to trim points and corners, grade seams, and clip curves.

TRIM POINTS AND CORNERS

Reinforce all points and corners with a second line of stitches directly over the first line. Trim the points and/or corners by trimming the seam allowances diagonally across the point or corner.

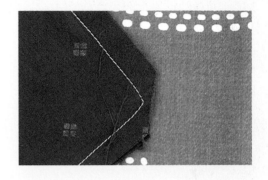

CLIP CURVES

On outside curves, such as inside a curved collar, clip several little V-shaped notches into the curved seam allowance. Doing so reduces the extra fabric in the seam allowance created by the inside curve so that when the curve is turned right side out, the Vs close up to make a smoother curve.

On inside curves, such as a neckline (as shown in the photo), make several little clips into the seam allowance, enabling the seam allowance to spread so that there are no puckers when it's turned right side out.

GRADE SEAMS

If your fabric is heavy or bulky, you will want to eliminate some of the bulk of the seam, especially on collars. This is called *layering* (or *grading*) *the seam allowance.*

There may be many seam allowances in the seam of a collar (for example, upper collar, interfacings, and under collar).

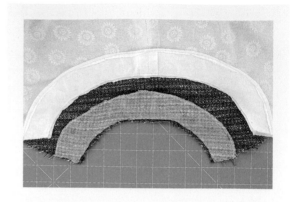

① To grade two layers, first trim the seam allowance of both by about half.

1

② Trim one of the two layers in half again. This makes the two layers different allowances, so that they lie more cleanly when the garment is turned right side out.

③ If there are more than two layers, trim the layers in various seam allowances, being careful not to cut into the actual seam.

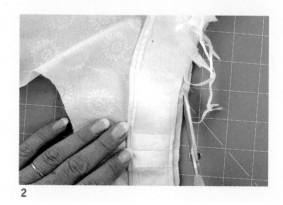

2

TIP

When layering, the layer that will be closest to the outside of the garment when it's turned right side out should be the longest to help camouflage the ridges from the other layered edges.

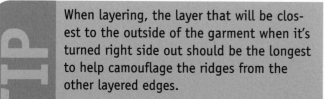

Embellishments

The number of possible embellishments available to home sewers is almost limitless. Some embellishments are functional, some are purely decorative, and some serve both purposes. The following are only a very few examples of what can be found in most fabric and craft stores.

TAPES AND RIBBONS

- **Bias tape** is cut on the bias and has give. It is used to finish curved edges. Double-fold bias tape can be stitched over the edges to be both functional and decorative. (Find more details for applying double-fold bias tape in Chapter 6.) Single-fold bias tape can be topstitched onto the right side of the fabric for a decorative element.

- **Seam binding** is used to finish hems and seams for its functional use. However, some seam binding has a lace design and can be topstitched onto the right side of a garment with some of the fabric under the lace trimmed away for a decorative effect.

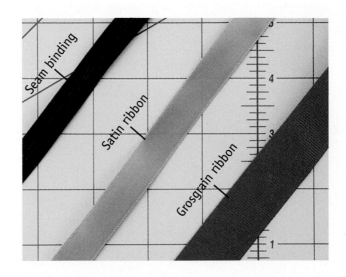

- **Woven jacquard ribbon** is used primarily as decoration and can be topstitched onto a garment.

- **Satin ribbon** is shiny and smooth, comes in an array of colors and widths, and is finished on both edges. You can zigzag over narrow satin ribbon with an invisible thread in the needle to stitch it onto a garment for decoration.

- **Grosgrain ribbon** comes in many colors and widths. It is finished on both edges and is identified by its prominent vertical lines. Grosgrain ribbon is often used as a belt or topstitched on for a waist decoration.

TRIMMINGS

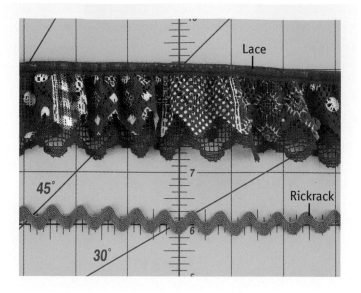

- **Lace** comes in a variety of designs, fabrics, colors, widths, and types. Some is finished on both edges, some is finished on only one edge, and some does not have either edge finished. Depending on the type of lace, it can either be topstitched onto a garment or be attached as an edge trim.

- **Rickrack** is primarily decorative and comes in a variety of colors and three different widths. It adds a decorative element when topstitched onto a garment or when used as an edge finish.

- **Finished piping** can be purchased already covered and ready to be inserted into a seam. It is easier to pin the piping first to the right sides of one of the garment pieces with the piping itself extending past the ⅝-inch seam allowance onto the fabric piece. The stitching on the piping seam allowance should be on top of the ⅝-inch seam allowance. Use either a piping foot, if you have one, or a zipper foot to stitch close to the piping. Then lay the second garment piece right sides together over the first garment piece and piping. Pin. Continuing to use either the zipper or piping foot, stitch the two pieces together on the ⅝-inch seam allowance.

- **Sequins in a strip** are purely decorative and are easily sewn onto a garment by hand or machine.

- **Beads in a strip** are decorative and easily sewn onto a garment by hand or machine.

APPLIQUÉS

Manufactured appliqués can be sewn on by hand using the slip stitch or by machine using the satin stitch. To create the satin stitch on your machine, set the zigzag width to an appropriate width for your appliqué and the stitch length as close to 0 as you can while still having some forward movement. You want the stitches to be very close together to cover the edge of the appliqué.

IRON-ON TRANSFERS

Many companies produce images of various kinds that you can iron onto T-shirts, jackets, blouses, pants, and other garments. Check your fabric store or online for ideas. To apply them, follow the instructions that come with the transfers.

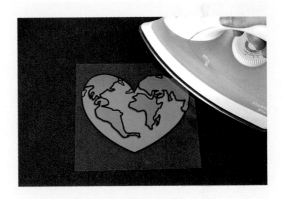

FYI

Computer-Generated Iron-ons

All major computer printer companies have a line of computer-generated iron-ons. It's easy to transfer pictures of your favorite people onto your T-shirt. Each manufacturer of iron-on transfers has slightly different directions. When purchasing transfer sheets, find the kind appropriate for your printer—inkjet or laser. Follow the instructions that come with the transfer sheets.

CHAPTER 3

Sewing from a Pattern

All manufactured sewing patterns are essentially the same—the pattern symbols, the design of the envelope, and the directions. Some of the newer independent pattern manufacturing companies have added their own unique look, but the basics remain unchanged. There are also Web sites that offer a variety of patterns for download. Sewing from a pattern is easy once you learn about and become familiar with the markings on the patterns and the information on the envelope.

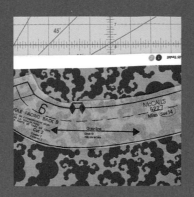
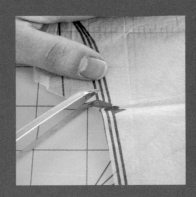

Find Patterns

Patterns can be found in many places. The most obvious place is a fabric store or a chain store that sells fabric. Tag sales and garage sales are great sources, too. Some churches and other community groups have fabric and sewing notion exchanges. And, of course, you can always set up a pattern swap with your friends. Several companies publish magazines that you can subscribe to or buy in any bookstore. Another relatively recent addition to the list of pattern sources is the Internet. This list includes many traditional pattern companies (such as Simplicity), independent companies, and individual designers, eBay and other auction sites, and patternmaking software.

Pattern Books

All fabric stores and some large chain stores that carry fabric have a section set aside for you to browse through pattern books. The books are color coded and arranged by style or garment—for example, casual wear or dresses. There are also specialty books (or sections of pattern books), such as bridal wear and children's fashions. Each company's pattern book displays hundreds of different patterns. Some books set aside sections for beginning sewers. These sections may be labeled "In an Hour," "Easy," and so on.

Some of the newer, smaller, independent pattern companies use pattern display racks rather than traditional pattern books or sell almost exclusively online. These display racks can be found near the pattern book area.

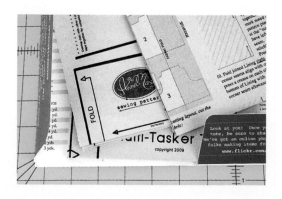

Patterns in pattern books change with the seasons. New patterns are added and older ones are discontinued. So if you don't find the kind of pattern you're looking for, try again later.

Pattern books are filled with useful information. The finished garment is pictured in a variety of fabrics. The book also displays the many variations you can make from one pattern. For example, a single pattern might include a top with or without sleeves, a pair of pants, a pair of shorts, and a skirt. For each pattern, there is also a line drawing of the front and back of each garment and a chart that suggests the amount of fabric needed for each garment and size.

Some patterns have little circles, hourglasses, triangles, and rectangles in the corners of the pages. These symbols correspond to common body shapes. For example, if you have an hourglass shape and you see an hourglass in the corner of a pattern, then that particular garment should look good on you.

Hourglass
Shoulders and hips
the same.
Waist = 10" smaller

Triangle
Shoulders narrower
than hips

Inverted Triangle
Upper body wider
than hips

Rectangle
Little or no waist
indentation

FYI

If the pattern you really want doesn't have your shape as a suggestion, don't worry. By following some of the suggestions in Chapter 4, you will be able to adapt the pattern to your body type.

Online

You can also find patterns on the Internet, some free to download and some for purchase. Many pattern companies offer online patterns for you to buy and/or download. In addition, many independent designers have begun printing innovative patterns and selling them on their blogs or websites. This is a great way to get up-to-the-minute designs. Some offer free patterns, others offer patterns for a nominal fee, and some do both.

If it's difficult for you to get to a good fabric store, downloading patterns or buying print patterns online are great alternatives. Here is a selection of some sites you may want to visit. Of course, there are many more.

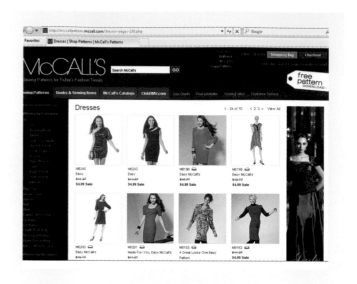

www.burdastyle.com/patterns
www.freeneedle.com
www.mccall.com (includes Vogue)
www.purlsoho.com
www.sewingpatterns.com
www.simplicity.com
www.sovintagepatterns.com

When you download and print a pattern on 8½-x-11-inch paper, you can end up with many pieces of paper, some with maybe one dot or a tiny segment of one line. Printing a pattern from the Internet adds the challenge of putting all the 8½-x-11-inch pieces of paper together. If you don't like puzzles, this probably isn't the place to begin; you instead might want to purchase paper patterns online. Familiarize yourself with the tried-and-true printed patterns from major pattern companies first, and then venture forth. Once you're familiar with the traditional markings on pattern pieces and know what to look for on the envelope, negotiating the myriad of options available via the Internet will be easier.

If you're new to fashion sewing, look through the easy section of a pattern book for an easy pattern—one with few pieces and few design details. When you find a style that appeals to you, read the list of recommended fabrics and check out the yardage for your size. Keep in mind the cost of the fabric per yard multiplied by how many yards you will need.

Size

Remember that not all size 8 people are the same and that the pattern size will not necessarily be the same as your ready-to-wear garment size. Pattern companies and designers try to design to the average. The problem is that not many of us are average. Size designations are somewhat arbitrary and keep changing over time. If you think you are a size 6 and the sizing on the pattern suggests you select a size 12, don't be depressed. They're only numbers! Remember, Marilyn Monroe is said to have been a size 12.

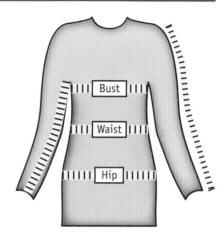

To select the correct size, measure yourself in the undergarments you usually wear and write down the following measurements:

- Bust at the widest point

- Waist

- Hip

Try not to pull the measuring tape too tight; you want the garment you spend hours making to fit you.

When you look at a pattern, check your measurements against what is listed in the chart to find the size that's closest to your own measurements. Don't be surprised if your measurements don't line up with the chart. For blouses, tops, and most dresses, select the pattern size closest to your bust measurement. If it's not exact, take the next size up. Taking in a garment is easier than letting it out.

For skirts and pants, select the size that most closely matches your waist or hips. For fitted skirts and pants, choose the hip measurement. For flowing skirts, choose the waist measurement. The reality is that you aren't going to find the perfect size on the chart. The pattern is only a general guide—all the adjustments that will make this garment uniquely yours will be made later.

In some cases, you might need different sizes for tops and bottoms. Most patterns are printed with various sizes on one pattern piece, enabling you to combine different sizes for different parts of your body and individualize your fit. This feature permits more flexibility when selecting a pattern. The range of sizes is listed in the pattern book and also on the pattern.

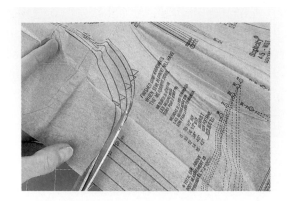

Fabric

Choosing the fabric for your pattern is part of the fun of making your own garments. However, all the different fabric and color choices can be overwhelming. Use your imagination. Will this garment look good on you in chartreuse or mauve? Pure cotton or acetate? Only you can decide. You will make mistakes, but that's part of the learning process.

In the pattern book and also on the pattern, the designer makes some suggestions for which fabric to choose for that style of garment (see the following section on how to read the pattern envelope). Check out these suggestions first. When you find the fabric, don't forget to read the end of the cardboard bolt to make sure that you're willing to follow the fabric care directions (see Chapter 1).

NOTE: Check your measurements against a pattern size every time you sew a new pattern. Each company or designer can size things a little differently, and even within pattern companies, sizing can change.

The Envelope

Pattern companies and designers put a great deal of information on the envelope to help you select an appropriate fabric and notions, such as buttons and/or zippers, and purchase the right amount of fabric. Read everything on the envelope before you decide to purchase the pattern.

FRONT

Most pattern envelopes from traditional patternmakers follow a standard layout and size:

1 Pattern company or designer

2 Pattern number

3 Size range

4 Garment in various fabrics

5 Letter indicating variations available (called *views*)

BACK

The back of the envelope lists everything you need to purchase to assemble the garment, often including:

1 Fabric suggestions

2 Body measurements

3 Views

4 Garment measurements

5 Diagrams

6 Fabric needed in English units

7 Fabric needed in metric units

8 Notions

9 Information in Spanish

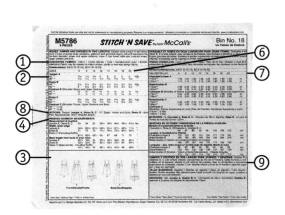

What's in the Envelope

Once you take everything out of the envelope, it may be difficult to get everything back in. Find a zippered plastic bag to store all the pieces. Cut the pattern envelope so that the front and back are separated. On the inside of the plastic bag, tape the front of the envelope (picture facing out) to one side of the plastic bag and the back of the envelope (back facing out) to the other side. Some people do get them folded and back into the envelope, but a lot of sewers can't or don't want to take the time.

PATTERN PIECES

In the envelope are two different kinds of paper. One type contains the pattern pieces. There are often many very large sheets of tissue paper that have several different pattern pieces printed on them; these sheets might seem unwieldy.

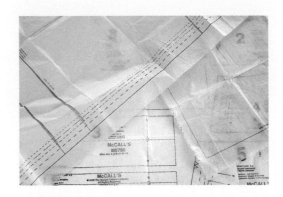

DIRECTION SHEET

The other kind of paper contains the printed step-by-step instructions along with a few other helpful bits of information about the pattern.

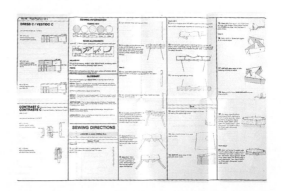

SKETCH

You will often find a line drawing for each of the gar-ments in the pattern envelope. This sketch will give you a clearer idea of where darts, tucks, zippers, seams, and other design features go.

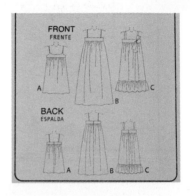

NUMBERED PIECES

Each pattern piece is numbered sequentially and dia-grammed. In the accompanying list, the pieces are listed with their numbers and also with letters indicating which view each piece goes with.

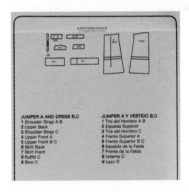

GENERAL DIRECTIONS

In the general directions, general sewing techniques, plus some specialized techniques for this particular pat-tern, are briefly described.

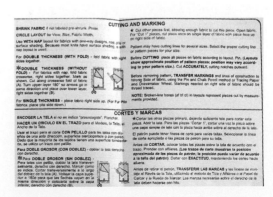

CUTTING LAYOUT

The cutting layout page suggests how to lay the pattern pieces on the fabric. Fabrics come in two widths: 42–45 inches and 56–60 inches, plus or minus a few inches. (Felt, some fleece, sheeting, and decor fabrics are usually wider.) Various factors can affect layout. Sometimes the fabric's fold is crosswise; other times, it's longwise. The fabric may have nap (see Chapter 2) and require the top of each pattern piece to be laid in the same direction. The size of your garment—whether it's a 6 or a 16—also determines how the pattern pieces are to be arranged for cutting. These layouts are designed to minimize how much fabric you will need. They will save you time in fitting all the pattern pieces on the fabric.

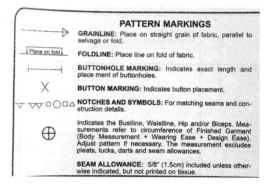

SYMBOLS AND MARKINGS

In this section is a list and description of the symbols and markings you find on the pattern pieces, such as dots, grainline, button and buttonholes, and notches. (See "Mark and Cut" later in this chapter.)

PATTERN MARKINGS

GRAINLINE: Place on straight grain of fabric, parallel to selvage or fold.

FOLDLINE: Place line on fold of fabric.

BUTTONHOLE MARKING: Indicates exact length and place ment of buttonholes.

BUTTON MARKING: Indicates button placement.

NOTCHES AND SYMBOLS: For matching seams and construction details.

Indicates the Bustline, Waistline, Hip and/or Biceps. Measurements refer to circumference of Finished Garment (Body Measurement + Wearing Ease + Design Ease). Adjust pattern if necessary. The measurement excludes pleats, tucks, darts and seam allowances.

SEAM ALLOWANCE: 5/8" (1.5cm) included unless otherwise indicated, but not printed on tissue.

SEWING DIRECTIONS

The step-by-step directions for assembling your garment fill the rest of the pages. Notice that the directions for the different views may start in different places in the directions. If more than one garment is included in the envelope, the directions for each garment will start in different places. It might be helpful to circle the directions for the view and garment you are making.

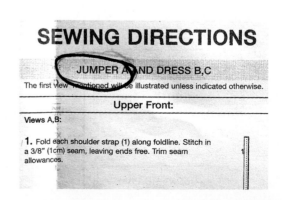

SEWING DIRECTIONS

JUMPER A AND DRESS B,C

The first view mentioned will be illustrated unless indicated otherwise.

Upper Front:

Views A,B:

1. Fold each shoulder strap (1) along foldline. Stitch in a 3/8" (1cm) seam, leaving ends free. Trim seam allowances.

Pattern Pieces

1. On the direction sheet where the numbered pieces are shown and listed, circle the ones you need.

2. Decide on the size you will be making.

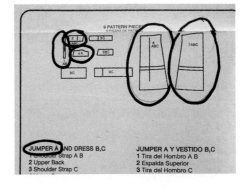

3. See Chapter 4 on fitting your pattern first, then cut out all the pattern pieces on the line designated for your size. Some lines are solid, some are just dots, and some are dashed lines. When you come to a choice, cut on the lines for the size you decided on in Step 2.

4. Put the pieces you don't need for this project in the plastic bag (see page 68).

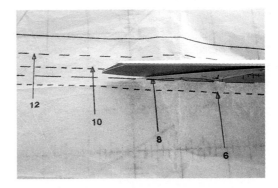

5. Sometimes the different-sized pieces such as facings are printed separately. Find the ones you need.

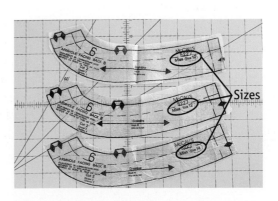

Adjust the Length of Pattern Pieces

If you have to lengthen or shorten any part of a garment, lines on the pattern indicate where this should be done. Be sure to adjust all the corresponding pattern pieces the same amount, including the linings! Make all adjustments to the pattern pieces before you place the pieces on the fabric for cutting. Otherwise, you may forget and cut the fabric in the wrong place.

SHORTENING

Fold the pattern with an accordion pleat half the amount needed to shorten (since the pleat is double, an inch pleat would make the pattern a total of 2 inches shorter overall), keeping the lines parallel and the grainline arrow straight. Pin in place.

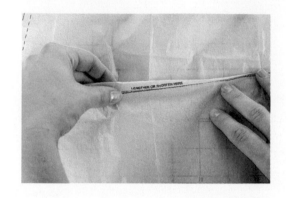

LENGTHENING

Cut the pattern piece where indicated. Pull the pattern pieces apart equal to the amount of length that needs to be added. Place a piece of paper underneath the cut and tape the paper to both parts of the pattern piece. Keep the lines parallel and the grainline arrow straight.

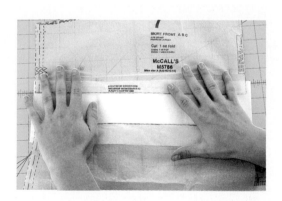

TIP

Because of the shape of certain pattern pieces, you can't just cut off the bottom or add length to the bottom without distorting the shape or design of the garment.

Put the Pattern on the Fabric

The most important step to remember when laying out a pattern is to pay attention to the grainlines. On each pattern piece is a line with an arrowhead on either end. This line (also called the straight-of-grain line) should be placed parallel to the selvage. (See Chapter 2 for more on grain and selvage.)

Fold Carefully

① Fold the fabric either lengthwise or widthwise as suggested on the pattern layout diagram. You need two of most pattern pieces (that is, two sleeves); with fabric folded, they can be cut at the same time. Be sure the selvages are parallel and there are no wrinkles along the folded edge. Slide the selvages back and forth until the fabric lies flat.

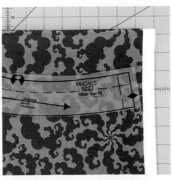

Fabric folded incorrectly

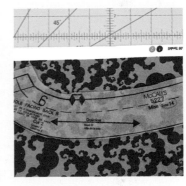

Fabric folded correctly

② Following the suggestion on the pattern layout diagram, lay all the pieces on the fabric to make sure they will all fit. Some pieces may say, "Place on fold." That fold line of the pattern piece should be placed exactly on the fold of the fabric. When these pieces are exactly on the fold and smooth, you can pin them in place.

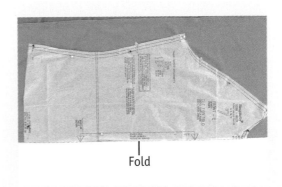

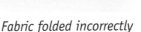

Fold

73

③ For other pattern pieces that are not on the fold and have a straight of grainline and arrowhead, measure with a ruler to determine the distance between the selvage and one of the arrowheads. Pin the pattern to the fabric at the arrowhead. Measure and adjust the line so that the other arrowhead is the same distance from the selvage. You may have to adjust the first pin until the line is perfectly parallel to the selvage. Pin that pattern piece in place.

Continue adjusting and pinning the rest of the pattern pieces so that they are on the straight of grain.

TIP

When pinning the pattern to the fabric, place the pins in the seam allowance and parallel to the cut edge.

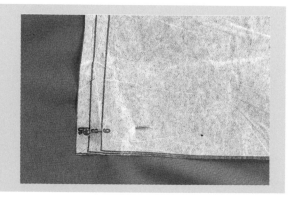

Mark and Cut

Use the marking method of your choice to transfer all the markings from the pattern to the fabric. (For more on marking, see Chapter 2.) Notches and dots are two of the most common symbols used by pattern companies.

Notches

Notches are used to match edges that are going to be seamed together. There are either one, two, or three notches together. Note that the single notch placement in the photo varies a little for the different size patterns.

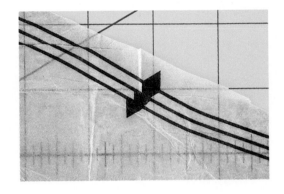

The terminology on the pattern directions will say, "Match the notches." You match one notch with one notch, two notches with two notches, and so on. On a sleeve, for example, one notch on the armhole edge of the piece will be sewn to one notch on the *front* of the top, and two notches on the armhole edge of the piece will be sewn to the two notches on the *back* of the top. If you mix this up, some sleeves won't fit correctly!

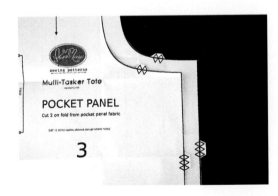

There are several methods of marking notches:

- Cut out around the notches, making your cuts accurate enough so that you can tell the difference between one, two, and three notches.

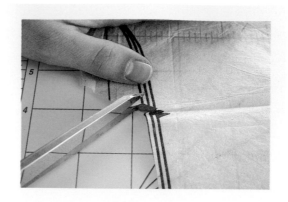

- With a marking pencil or pen and in the seam allowance, indicate with a straight line where the notches are.

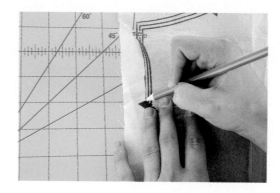

- In the seam allowance, snip about $3/8$ inch in from the edge where the notches are—one snip for each notch—being careful not to clip too deeply into the seam.

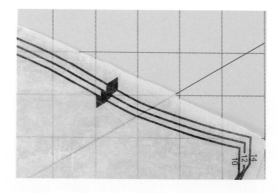

Dots

Dots mark a variety of important points on a pattern—for example, the top center of a sleeve that will be matched with the shoulder seam.

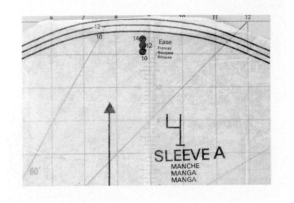

Top of sleeve dot matches shoulder seam.

Darts, pleats, and tucks are also marked with dots.

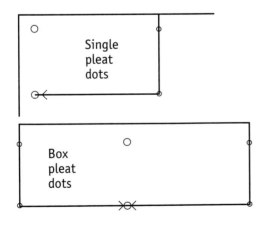

Single pleat dots

Box pleat dots

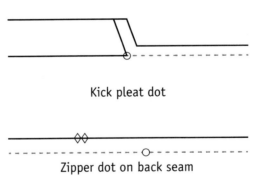

Kick pleat dot

Zipper dot on back seam

To mark the dots on the fabric, you can use tailor tacks (see Chapter 2).

Alternatively, you can use a marking pencil or pen.

Be sure to mark on the wrong side of the fabric with a marker that will not show through to the right side.

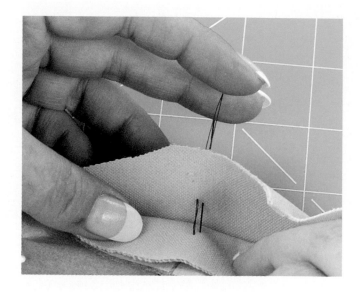

*Tailor tacks are one way to transfer dots
on the pattern to the fabric*

A host of patternmaking software is available to computer-savvy sewers. Because you enter all your measurements into the program, the pattern that's printed is designed just for your body. You don't have to worry about making alterations to the pattern as you would on a commercially prepared pattern.

Some patternmaking software enables you to select from many options for length, style, shape, sleeves, openings, and so on. The possibilities are almost infinite. As with patterns that you download, you end up printing a great many pages with not much on them that you need to tape together.

Two patternmaking software examples are:

www.livingsoftnw.com
www.wildginger.com

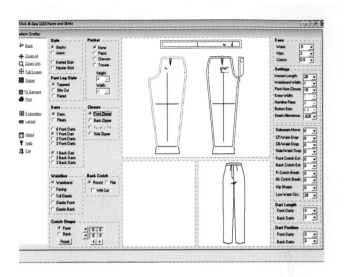

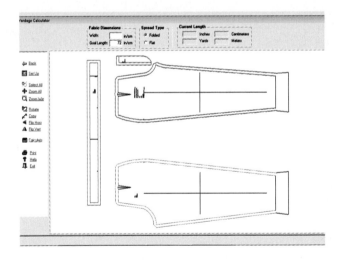

CHAPTER 4

Find the Right Fit

Because there are an infinite number of body sizes and shapes and only a few pattern sizes and shapes, you almost certainly will not be able to find a pattern that fits you perfectly. Pattern manufacturers design their patterns based on their idea of the size and shape of the "average" person. They assign a size number, but that number is relative only to their other size numbers. In addition, you may be one size on top and a different size on the bottom.

Invariably, you will have to adjust patterns to fit you. Being able to make the adjustments needed to get a good-fitting garment is one of the reasons to sew clothes yourself. We are more comfortable, are more confident, and look better when we know that our garments fit and flatter us.

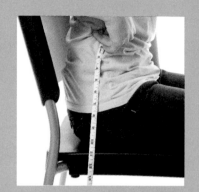
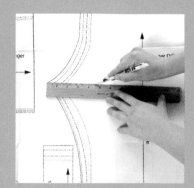

Use a Paper Pattern to Make Alterations

Whether you make your own patterns, purchase them, or download them, you will likely need to adjust the pattern to get a perfect fit for your unique body. This chapter provides suggestions and techniques for altering dresses, pants, skirts, and tops. In general, the processes are the same. You may need to lengthen or shorten, or increase or decrease the size of a garment. Most alterations can be accomplished in the seam lines or the shaping features—darts, pleats, and gathers.

Get Out Your Pattern Pieces

After purchasing a pattern that suits your basic shape at the size closest to your measurements, you must decide which size within the pattern envelope you need. Most patterns cover a range of sizes; this is called *multisizing*. If your measurements indicate that you need one size in the bust, another size in the waist, and yet another size in the hips, multisized patterns are very helpful because you can gradually change from one size line to the next.

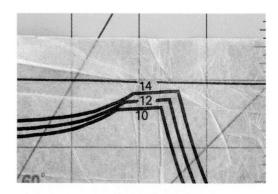

1 Find the main pattern pieces for the garment you want to make. Remember from Chapter 3 that the direction sheet in the pattern envelope lists all the pattern pieces and their purposes. You don't need the facings, waistbands, embellishments, or pockets at this time. You do, however, need at least the front and back pieces. For dresses and tops, include the sleeves.

2 Cut out these pieces on the biggest size line on the pattern.

Try on the Paper Pattern

Pin the major pattern pieces together as they would be joined in construction, along the seam line of the size that your measurements indicate you need. Because most pattern pieces are cut on double fabric, what you have pinned together will no doubt cover just half of your body. This is enough to get a general idea of which areas will need alterations.

Check to see that the seam line for the center-front and center-back pieces comes to the center of your body all the way up and down. If it doesn't come to the center of your body in the hip area, let out the pins on the side seams and try the next larger size.

If, for a dress, blouse, or other top, the seam line doesn't come to the middle of your center front in the bust area, you'll probably need to do a bust alteration (see following page).

NOTE: The major pattern companies size their misses patterns for a B cup.

Before you do the bust alterations, check the shoulder seams and adjust them as needed. The seam should be perpendicular to the arm at the shoulder. It also may need to be pulled up to make the armhole smaller or the seam let out to make the armhole bigger.

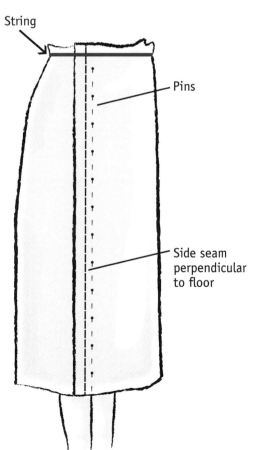

String

Pins

Side seam perpendicular to floor

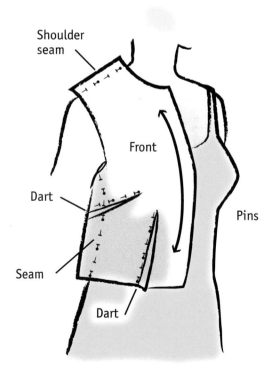

Shoulder seam

Front

Dart

Pins

Seam

Dart

Bust Alterations

INCREASE SIZE

To increase the size of a darted blouse, jacket, or dress bodice for a large bust:

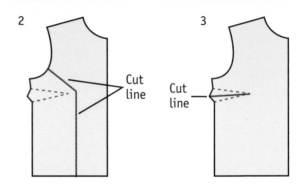

1. Unpin the front bodice pattern piece and lay it on top of a large piece of paper.

2. Cut your pattern (but not the paper under it) in a straight line from the waist up to the bust point, and then angle up to (but not through) the seam line at the arms notch.

3. Cut a second line from the side seam through the bust dart almost to—but not through—the bust point.

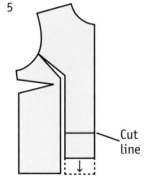

4. Pull the lower side seam down and out so that the vertical opening slit is about ½ inch wide, increasing the cup size from a B to a C.

5. Steps 3 and 4 make the side-front part of the pattern a little longer than the center-front section, so cut a horizontal slit across the center-front pattern piece and pull it straight down to equal the lower edge of the side front.

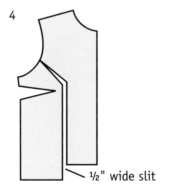

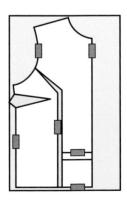

6. Tape the spread pattern onto the paper below and draw lines along the edges to connect the slit areas. Cut out your new bodice front pattern piece with these alterations made.

DECREASE SIZE

To decrease the size of a darted blouse, jacket, or dress bodice for a small bust:

1 Cut the pattern in the same manner as if increasing size (steps 1–5 above), but overlap the pattern pieces instead of spreading them.

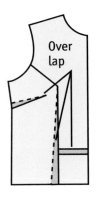

Over lap

2 After decreasing the bust area, pin the darts back in and pin the side and shoulder seams again.

3 Try on the bodice pattern pieces to see if this alteration helped bring the center front of the pattern over to your center front in the bust area and bring the point of the bust darts to the pointy part of your bust.

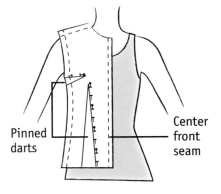

Pinned darts

Center front seam

TIP

If the neckline gaps, take a ¼- to ½-inch horizontal tuck in the neckline that tapers to nothing at the armhole.

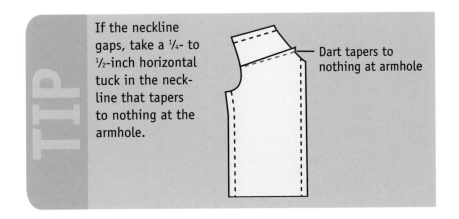

Dart tapers to nothing at armhole

Lengthen or Shorten the Pattern

While you have the paper pattern on, check to see that the marking for the waistline on a dress bodice, jacket, or blouse falls at your natural waistline. It may need to be shortened or lengthened. Also check the overall length of a dress or skirt to see if it needs to be shortened or lengthened. See Chapter 3 for more on how to lengthen or shorten a paper pattern.

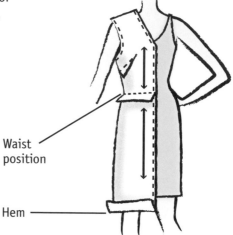

Waist position

Hem

If you make any of these alterations to your pattern, remember that you will also have to make the same alteration on the pattern piece that stitches to it. For example, if you add length to the skirt front, you'll need to add the same amount of length to the skirt back for the side seams to match. If you lengthen the bodice or make the full bust alteration, then you'll need to lengthen the front facing the same amount.

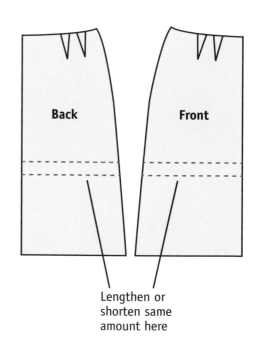

Back

Front

Lengthen or shorten same amount here

Alter Corresponding Pattern Pieces

FYI

There are other pieces to remember when altering a pattern. For example, a facing or interfacing may need to be changed. If you have altered the length of a dress or top that has darts that extend over the area lengthened or shortened, you will also have to change the darts.

*E*ase is the difference in size between the actual body measurements and the size of the pattern. You want your garments to have the right amount of ease so that they are comfortable to wear, but not so loose that they are unflattering.

There are two kinds of ease: wearing (or moving) ease and design ease.

Wearing ease is the extra amount added to the dimensions of a pattern so that you have room to move around and feel comfortable when you wear the garment.

Design ease is the extra amount the designer adds to the pattern for a particular style of garment. For example, a very full skirt is designed with a considerable amount of additional design ease beyond the basic wearing ease needed for a skirt. Similarly, a very loose-fitting over-blouse is designed with more design ease than a classic tailored blouse with darts.

Different fabrics require different amounts of ease. Basic ease for bust, waist, and hips are 2–3 inches, 1–1½ inches, and 1½–3 inches respectively. Some fabrics, such as spandex, fit better with a small amount of ease. Other heavier, stiffer fabrics that do not have much give fit better with more ease. In determining the amount of ease needed for the garment you're making, decide whether you want your garment to fit like paint, flow about in the breeze, or fall somewhere in between.

Little design ease

More design ease

Little design ease

More design ease

Make a Mock-up Muslin

After your paper fitting (see "Use a Paper Pattern to Make Alterations," earlier in this chapter), unpin the pattern pieces and use them to make a mock-up muslin test garment. This is helpful the first time you use a purchased pattern to sew a garment that fits close to the body, because the muslin will drape and hang better on your body than the stiff paper did. Making the muslin takes extra time, but in the end, having a garment that fits well is worth the effort.

Prep the Muslin

① For making mock-ups, purchase several yards of cheap muslin, or use old bed sheets.

② Press the muslin or sheeting. You don't need to pre-shrink it, though, because you will probably never wash it!

2

③ Pin the major pattern pieces to the muslin, following the layout suggested by the pattern. Make sure that the selvages of the fabric are parallel, the grainline of the pattern is on the straight-of-grain line of the fabric, and the folds are placed on folds.

3

Trace the Pattern and Cut Out the Pieces

① With a marking pen or carbon paper and tracing wheel, trace the pattern onto the muslin using the size lines you think will fit you.

② Trace all the other marks on the pattern: darts, center points, waistline, and zipper opening as shown in the photo. If you're new to sewing, you may want to trace the sewing lines, too.

③ Read the direction sheet to see whether the seam allowances suggested by this particular pattern are the standard ⅝ inch. Most patterns still use ⅝ inch as the standard, but some are moving to ½ inch. Mark the muslin accordingly.

④ Remove the paper pattern and cut out the muslin pieces along the marked lines.

2

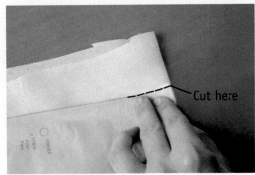

Cut here

4

Sew the Muslin Pieces Together

Sew the muslin pieces together by hand or machine using a long or basting stitch in a contrasting color thread, which makes it easier to pull out the threads and change them if you need to alter a seam. Be sure to sew on the seam allowance lines suggested or marked.

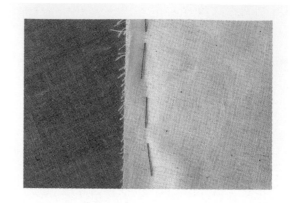

FOR A SKIRT

1. If there is a front seam, sew the front seam.

2. If there is a back seam with a zipper opening, sew the back seam up to the zipper opening. Do not sew the zipper opening shut.

3. Sew the front and back together at the side seams.

   Don't bother to sew darts, tucks, or anything else; just pin the darts or pleats in place.

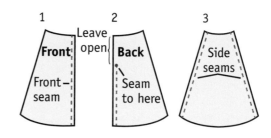

4. If there are gathers, sew a gathering line between the dots indicated.

5. Sew a line of basting stitches on the waistline sewing line.

6. Pin up the hem where you think you want the hem to be.

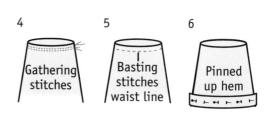

FOR A TOP

1. Baste the darts in place on the front and back pieces.

2. Baste the center front seam, if there is one.

3. Baste the center back seam, if there is one.

4. Baste the front to the back at the side seams.

5. Baste the shoulder seams.

6. On the sewing line, baste around the neck and armhole openings. In the seam allowance, clip just to the sewing line and pin to the inside.

7. On the pattern, there will be a mark that indicates the waistline. Baste, pin, or mark the line on the muslin.

8. Before adding sleeves, try on the muslin, making adjustments as needed and as suggested below.

9. When you are satisfied with the fit, baste on the sleeves. Adjust the sleeves accordingly. Lengthen or shorten the sleeves or add or subtract some fullness.

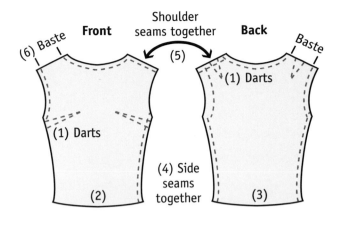

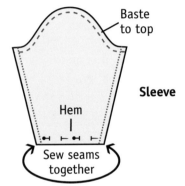

For a dress with a waistline seam, follow the suggestions for skirts and tops, but do not sew the waistline seam. When the alterations for the top and skirt of the dress are close to what you want, baste the top to the bottom. Try on the dress again, following the suggestions below for dresses without a waistline seam.

1. On the pattern there will be a mark that indicates the waistline. Baste, pin, or mark the line on the muslin.

2. Baste in the darts.

3. Baste in the front, back, and/or side seams, leaving the zipper/button opening open.

4. Baste the shoulder seams.

5. On the sewing line, baste around the neck and armhole openings. In the seam allowance, clip just to the sewing line and pin to the inside.

TRY IT ON

Put the mockup muslin garment on inside out. (You may need a friend to help you.) On a skirt, dress, or top with a zipper opening, pin the zipper opening closed on the sewing line. On a garment with buttons, pin the center front or back openings together.

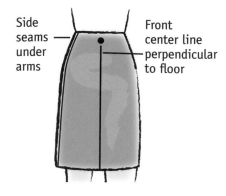

Side seams under arms

Front center line perpendicular to floor

Check the following:

1 The side seam lines should be under your arms, straight down your sides.

2 The center-front dot, front fold line, or front seam should be over your navel and straight down your center front, all the way up and down your body.

3 The darts should take in an appropriate amount of fabric so that no points are sticking out. On a top or dress, the bust point should not be too high or too low, and the darts point should end about 1 inch back away from the bust point.

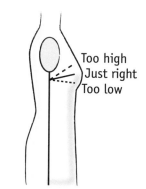

Too high
Just right
Too low

4 The side seams and darts should fit smoothly, with an amount of ease that feels comfortable to you.

5 There should be no wrinkles in the back darts. If necessary, have a friend adjust them for you.

6 The waistline line should be at your waistline. With the garment on, tie a narrow ribbon, elastic, or string around your waist. It should land on the waistline line that you drew. If it doesn't, lengthen or shorten the top accordingly.

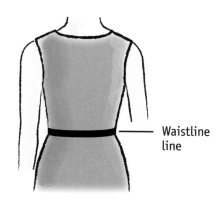

Waistline line

7. On a garment with princess lines (see Chapter 10), the seam should go directly over the bust, and both seam lines should be equidistant from the center-front lines.

8. On a dress with a waistline, the skirt darts and bust darts (if they start from the waist) should line up.

9. The hem length on a skirt and dress is where you want it to be.

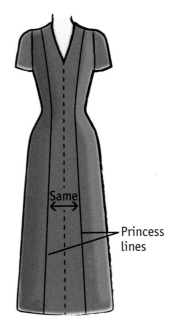

Same

Princess lines

Because this is a muslin that won't be worn, you can write your notes about necessary adjustments right on the muslin, such as "Add 1 inch to length." Or you could mark a new position for, say, the bust point. If the side seams need to be taken in, you can just pin them a little deeper; if they need to be let out, you can pull out the basting thread and pin the seam allowance narrower. If you change a seam allowance from the standard ⅝ inch, note it on the muslin or use a marking pen to mark where you have put the pins so that you can see them when you take off the muslin and separate the pieces.

NOTE: If you have to change any part by more than an inch or so, try a different size.

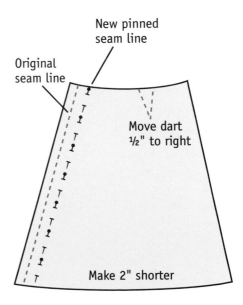

New pinned seam line

Original seam line

Move dart ½" to right

Make 2" shorter

TAKE THE MUSLIN GARMENT APART

When you're satisfied that the muslin pattern is exactly the way you want it, and you have clearly marked all the changes, take the muslin pattern pieces apart. Onto a large sheet of paper or your original pattern (if you haven't made too many big changes), trace the muslin pieces, remembering to mark all the new darts.

Label your new pattern pieces with the same numbers used on the original pattern pieces. This will be your new pattern.

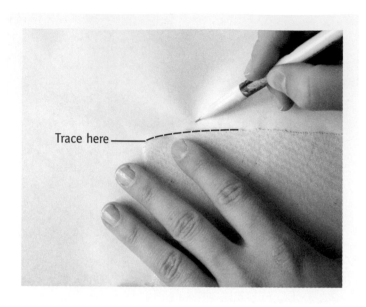

Trace here

If other pattern pieces—for example, the waistbands or facings—need to be altered, also make those changes to match the basic pieces. Transfer all the dots and notch markings. See "Using a Paper Pattern to Make Alterations," earlier in this chapter, for more on which other pieces might need to be altered.

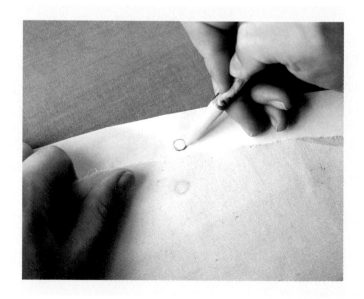

Even though you have measured and fitted your paper pattern and muslin, you still should double-check the fit of your garment periodically during construction because the fabric might give a little differently than the muslin. If you do a good job with the previous fitting steps, construction fitting changes should be minimal. Even if no changes need to be made, you can take comfort in knowing that the garment is going to fit you before you put time and effort into finishing it.

DRESS BODICES, BLOUSES, JACKETS, OR COATS

After you sew the side and shoulder seams and stitch any darts, try on the garment to make sure that:

- The side seams are straight.
- The center fold lines are straight down the center of your body.
- The darts fall in the right place.
- The waistline falls on your natural waistline.
- The shoulder seams go straight across your shoulders.

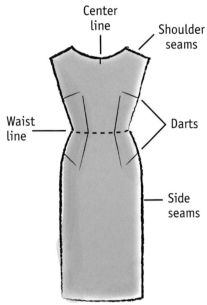

SKIRTS

After you stitch the side and back seams and any darts, try on the skirt to check:

- The fit of the hips.
- The side seams—they should be hanging straight.
- The placement of the darts.
- The placement of the waistline.

NOTE: Pants fitting is discussed in the following section.

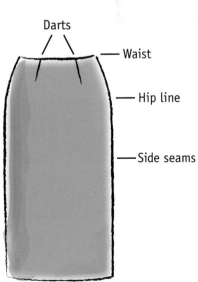

Before proceeding with construction, make any necessary adjustments to your garment, such as letting out or taking in side seams or taking out the stitching and moving a dart.

If you have made several changes, try on the garment again to make sure that these changes have given you the better fit that you desired.

Continue constructing your garment. Then try it on again at least one more time before you do any closures, such as buttons and snaps, and before you hem the garment.

Now you can take off the garment and feel confident in finishing a garment that will fit you.

TIP

Try on the garment with the shoes and undergarments you intend to wear with it. Stand in front of a mirror (or have a friend help you) to check that the hem is hanging straight and even all the way around, and that it is the length you want. (See Chapter 5 for more on hemming.)

Fitting pants differs from fitting dresses or skirts in that there are distinct areas that need to be measured. As discussed in Chapter 3, you need to take your waist and hip measurements when selecting a pattern size. For pants, you need at least three additional measurements: crotch depth, crotch length, and overall outseam leg length.

Crucial Pants Measurements

CROTCH DEPTH

To measure crotch depth:

1. Sit up straight on a straight chair and measure from your waist straight down your side to the chair.

2. To this measurement, add between ½ and 1 inch of wearing ease (see "What Is Ease?" earlier in this chapter), depending on the style of pants you are making and your personal preference for a snug or loose fit.

Often the crotch line is marked on the back pattern piece. If it is not marked:

1. Draw a line straight from the crotch point (the spot at which the seam line of the inseam and the center-back seam intersect) over to the side seam. This is the crotch line.

2. Measure straight down the side seam line on the pattern from the waist seam line to this crotch line to see if it equals your measurement from sitting on the chair plus your wearing ease. If, for example, your pattern is designed for the top of the pants to be 1 inch below the natural waistline, simply sub-tract 1 inch from the sitting measurement plus ease when you measure the pattern.

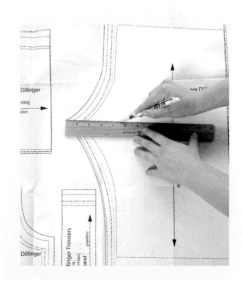

CROTCH LENGTH

To measure crotch length:

1 Put a tape measure through your legs, holding the end of the tape measure up to your center-back waist and pulling the other end up over your stomach to your center-front waist. Your crotch length is the figure where the tape measure meets your center-front waist.

2 Lay your front and back pattern pieces down with the crotches facing each other and the crotch point seam lines overlapping as they would be stitched. (This forms a U-shape for the crotch area.)

3 Holding your tape measure up on its side, measure on the seam line (not on the pattern edge) from the center-front waist seam line to the center-back waist seam line.

Compare this measurement to your crotch length measurement. Slide the pattern pieces together or apart until the measurement is the same as your crotch measurement.

NOTE: If your pattern is designed to be 1 inch below the natural waistline, subtract 1 inch from the front and back.

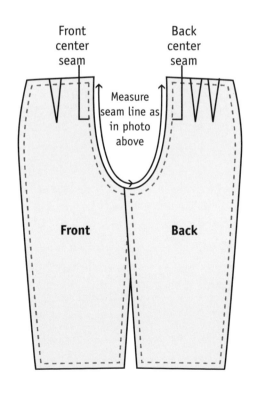

Front center seam

Back center seam

Measure seam line as in photo above

Front   Back

OUTSEAM

To take the outseam measurement for the overall length of your pants:

① Letting the end of the tape measure dangle down to your side, stand on the end of the tape with the 1-inch mark under your heel.

② Pull the tape measure up to your waist or 1 inch down for a dropped waist pattern. The number where the tape measure meets your waist is the overall length of your pants, which includes a hem allowance of 2 inches (since you stood with the 1-inch mark under your heel and measured from the floor rather than from where the bottom of your hem would be).

③ Measure straight down near the side seam of your paper pattern to compare this measurement to your outseam. You can make adjustments to lengthen or shorten your pants on the lengthen/shorten marking line on both the front and back pattern pieces between the knee and the ankle.

NOTE: If you're making a shorter style of pants, such as capris, measure how much shorter you want them to be than a regular pair of pants. Subtract that amount from your standard outseam measurement and use the result for your new outseam measurement.

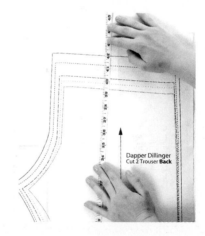

Dapper Dillinger
Cut 2 Trouser **Back**

TIP

You may need to add or subtract length from the center front, center back, or both depending on the following factors:

- **Full abdomen:** Add length to the top of the center-front seam.
- **Swayback:** Shorten the center-back seam.
- **Full seat:** Add length to the crotch point.
- **Flat seat:** Decrease the length of the crotch point.

THIGH AND LEG MEASUREMENTS

The thigh and leg area sometimes needs to be adjusted as well. If you have full thighs and legs, you can increase the leg width on the pattern about 1 to 2 inches below the crotch point and straighten the contour of the leg seams. If you have thin thighs and legs, you can decrease the width in the thigh and leg area. To determine whether you need to make pattern alterations in this area:

① Wrap a tape measure around the fullest part of your thigh. Add a minimum of 2 inches of wearing ease.

② Lay your paper pattern front and back pieces with the side seams overlapping on the seam line in the thigh area. Measure across both pattern pieces in the thigh area (about 1 to 2 inches below the crotch point). This measurement should be at least the measurement of your leg in the thigh area plus the 2 inches of ease.

Make a Pants Muslin

Because so many areas on a pair of pants are crucial to a good fit, it's helpful to make a muslin to see whether the alterations you made to the paper pattern give you the results you want. Follow the directions for marking the muslin and cutting out the pieces as outlined earlier in this chapter.

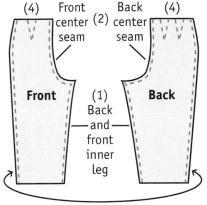

(3) Sew front and back together at side seams

1 With right sides together, baste front to back at inner leg seams.

2 Keeping right sides together, baste the remainder of the center crotch seam together, leaving any zipper opening open so that you can try the pants on.

3 Still with right sides together, baste the front to the back at the side seams.

4 Pin in any darts or pleats and pin up the hem.

5 Turn the muslin right side out, pin the hem allowance up, and try on the muslin. Tie a ¼-inch elastic around your waist (if the pants are designed with a natural waistline) to hold the pants in position while you check the fit.

PANTS FITTING CHECKLIST

- Stand in front of a full-length mirror (it helps to hold a hand mirror up also to check the back) and ascertain that the dart or pleat placement is appropriate and that the side seams hang straight.

- Check that there isn't any pulling, puckering, or bagginess in the hip, thigh, or crotch area.

- Tie a ¼-inch elastic around the waist and check the crotch length by pulling the top of the pants up more under the elastic if the crotch seems too low or pulling the top down if the crotch seems too high. Mark on the muslin where you adjust it under the elastic; this will be your new waistline seam line.

- Check the overall length of the pants and the fit at the waist.

- Hold up a hand mirror and check the fit of the back crotch when you turn your back to the full-length mirror. You can take in or let out any of the seams or darts as needed for a better fit. Another area that might need a slight alteration is the lower crotch curve area between the back and front notches, particularly if you have a low seat or if sideways wrinkles are showing just below the seat when you hold the mirror and look at your backside with the muslin on. The crotch curve can be lowered—that is, you can make the seam ¼ inch deeper and taper it back to the normal seam allowance at both the front and back notches. You then trim this lower crotch curve seam allowance between the two notches by ¼ inch so that the seam allowance is still ⅝ inch. Try on the muslin again and see if that helped the fit. Remember to mark with a marking pen on the muslin any changes you have made.

- Sit down in the pants to make sure there is room in the seat area and the crotch curve is adequate for you to sit comfortably without the waist pulling down in the back.

You're now ready to take your muslin pieces apart and transfer any changes to your paper pattern or use your muslin to draw a new paper pattern if you have made several big changes. Be sure to transfer all dots and markings.

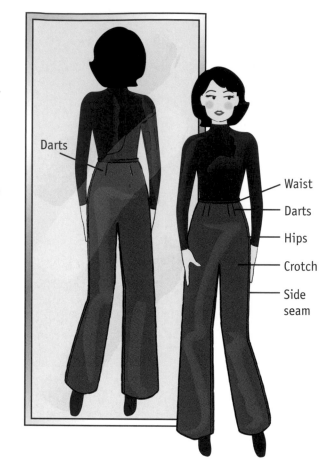

Darts

Waist

Darts

Hips

Crotch

Side seam

Fitting Pants during Construction

When making pants, you usually start by putting in any darts or pleats and any inseam or slant pockets. Stitch the side seams, inseams, and crotch seams together with the regular stitch length in the order outlined in the previous section on constructing a muslin, noting if a zipper goes in the side seam or the back.

NOTE: If you're putting in a regular zipper, apply the seam finishes but leave that area open. If you're inserting an invisible zipper, you will need to put it in before sewing the seam (see "Zippers" in Chapter 2), so leave the whole seam open for now and pin it together so that you can try on the pants.

Turn your pants right side out and try them on to check the fit. Again, tie a $\frac{1}{4}$-inch elastic around your waist and pin up the hem allowance for a better picture of the fit. Look for wrinkles, which would indicate excess fabric that needs to be taken up, or puckers or pulling, which would indicate that an area needs to be let out. Follow the checklist in the previous section on making a pants muslin, and make any necessary adjustments.

When you're satisfied with the fit (sometimes with pants it takes many repetitions of trying them on and making adjustments), continue to construct your pants with the zipper and waistband (see chapters 2 and 6, respectively, for more information). Before you do the closures and hemming, try them on again and double-check the back view and the fit of the crotch area.

CHAPTER 5

Hems and Hemlines

The hem is traditionally at the bottom of a garment or parts of a garment, such as sleeves and pant legs. Hems are usually just functional, but they can sometimes be decorative as well.

In years past, hemlines on dresses and skirts were at a fixed distance from the floor. This distance changed with the decades, and hemlines floated up and down. Today, you decide how long you want your skirts and pants to be. We are in a time of no rules. Anything goes!

There are many ways to do a hem. Even if your pattern suggests one particular way, you are free to choose whichever way you want to do it.

Before you begin to hem, you need to even the bottom of your garment all around, and make sure the edges are finished so they do not ravel. Then you need to determine the width and type of hem you want. Finally, you need to decide how you want to put in your hem. There are three basic mechanisms by which a hem can be put in: by hand, by machine, or by fusing.

TRIM AND FINISH

❶ Before you begin to hem, trim the bottom edge of your garment so that it is even all around, especially at the seam ends.

❷ Edge finish the raw edge on most fabrics to keep the hem edge from raveling.

NOTE: Knits that do not ravel do not need an edge finish. You also do not need to finish the edge if you sew a double-fold hem, because the first fold acts as the finish. Various edge finishes are listed in the hem instructions that follow. (For more about edge finishing, see Chapter 2.)

WIDTH, TYPE, AND METHOD

❶ Determine the width of hem you need to give you the desired garment length. While standing in front of a mirror, try on the garment with the hem pinned up the amount the pattern recommends so that you can see if that is the length that you want.

❷ Decide the type of hem you want (single fold, double fold, and so forth), if you have not already (see "Double-Fold Hems" and "Single-Fold Hems" later in this chapter). Also decide which of the following methods of hemming (see the next page) is the most appropriate for the style of garment and fabric with which you are working.

HAND STITCH

There are several different stitches that you can use to stitch a hem by hand. However, when you stitch a hem by hand, you should not be able to see the stitches on the public (right) side of the garment. If the stitches are visible, they are tiny and evenly spaced.

MACHINE STITCH

Using your machine to make the blind hem stitch will also make some tiny, evenly spaced stitches that show on the right side. Other machine-stitched hems will show a line of stitching on the right side and can be simply functional or also decorative.

FUSE THE HEM

Fused hems are made by using your steam iron to provide heat, steam, and pressure to melt the fusible web that fuses the hem to the garment. Therefore, a fused hem does not have any stitches showing on the right side.

TIP

Before fusing your hem, test the fusible web on a scrap of fabric to make sure that the amount of heat required to fuse the web does not damage the fabric. Even though the package says "permanent," some fusible webs do not last through many washings and a great deal of wear and tear. Fusible web is great for temporary fixes, however.

Double-Fold Hems

Double-fold hems are among the most common types of hem finishes, and there are several ways to create this kind of hem. *Double-fold* means just that—two folds. You make a double-fold hem to prevent fraying and to keep the inside of a garment looking tidy.

Wide Double-Fold Hems

The wide double-fold hem is the traditional hem used most often for hemming woven fabric dresses, skirts, slacks, jackets, and some blouses.

1. Press the bottom (raw) edge to the inside ¼ inch. Alternatively, rather than folding, finish this edge by pinking or serging. If you want to better secure the first fold, topstitch close to the folded edge. That is fold 1. This fold is your edge finish.

2. Measure and press the folded edge to the inside by whatever width you determined your hem needed to be to give the look that you want as described earlier, in the introductory paragraph. That is fold 2.

3. Pin fold 1 to the wrong side of the garment, matching the seam lines.

BLIND STITCHING

1. To blind-stitch fold 1 to the garment by hand, thread a needle with a single thread knotted at the end. Start where you can take a stitch in the seam allowance to help hide the thread knot.

2 Working from right to left, take a stitch in the hem; slide the needle through the fold for about ½ inch; bring it back out of the fold; take a tiny stitch in the garment, grabbing only one or two threads of the garment; and bring the stitch up through the edge of the fold. Again, slide the needle and thread through the fold for about ½ inch, back out, and again take a tiny stitch, picking up only a thread or two of the garment. For more on blind stitching, see Chapter 2.

3 Continue on around the hem. Try to keep the stitches small and evenly spaced.

You can blind-stitch fold 1 to the garment by machine, if your machine has a blind hem foot and blind hem stitch setting. To use them to make a machine blind hem, follow the directions in your manual for your particular machine.

TOPSTITCHING
You could also topstitch fold 1 to the garment. Remember that if you topstitch from the wrong side of the garment, the bobbin stitches will show on the right side of the garment, so pick the color of your thread accordingly. (See Chapter 2 for more details on topstitching.)

Narrow Double-Fold Hems

This is often called a *shirt-tail hem* since it is quite often used to hem men's shirts. It is also used to hem ladies' blouses and very full skirts.

1 Press the bottom edge to the inside ¼ inch. That is fold 1. This will serve as the edge finish.

2 Press the folded edge in the inside another ¼ or ½ inch. That is fold 2.

3 Either blind-stitch by hand (as described under "Wide Double-Fold Hems," earlier) or machine-topstitch fold 1 to the garment as described in Chapter 2 (and shown in the photo).

TIP

If you topstitch, the bobbin stitches will show on the right side of the garment, so pick the color of your thread accordingly.

Curved Double-Fold Hems

Flared skirts and pant legs (which are wider at the bottom than where the top of the hem will be) require an extra step. If you plan on a wide hem, do the following:

1 Machine-baste, with a longer stitch length, a ¼-inch single-fold hem to the inside.

2 Pin fold 2 in place where you want it, at the second fold edge.

3 Match the seams.

4 Pin the top of the hem in place matching seams and centers of each section of the garment. Pull the basting thread to gather up and ease in the excess fabric so that the hem allowance lies flat on the flared garment.

5 Hand stitch in place with the catch stitch rather than the blind stitch, because the fold will be slightly gathered.

NOTE: The wider the hem, the more excess fabric you will have to gather. Consider making the hems on fuller skirts narrower.

CATCH STITCH

The catch stitch looks similar to an X. It should not be pulled tightly—it needs to be loose enough for the hem to have some give and movement.

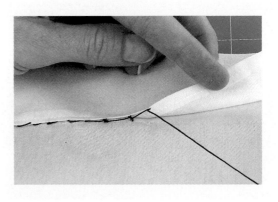

1 Thread, knot, and anchor the needle as described for hand blind stitch, earlier. From your first anchored stitch in one of the seam allowances, pull the thread back toward you and hold the thread under your left thumb.

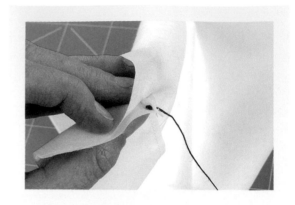

2 Take a tiny stitch straight through the hem allowance near the stitching on fold 1 and about ¼ inch to the right of your first stitch with your needle going away from you, again pulling the thread back toward you, and holding it under your left thumb.

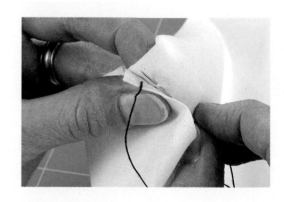

3 Moving to the right again about ¼ inch, run your needle (going away from you) under just one or two threads of your garment, slightly above the hem edge.

Repeat pulling the thread back toward you and under your left thumb, alternately stitching away from you on the hem allowance and on the garment, forming an X design.

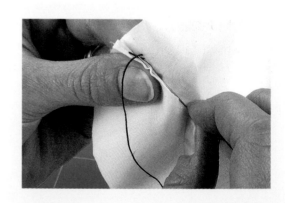

If you are making a garment out of a heavy fabric, double-fold hems are bulky. There are several single-fold hems you can use to eliminate bulk and keep the hem from fraying.

HEM WITH SEAM BINDING

Seam binding comes in a variety of colors and laces. It does not stretch like bias tape, and both long edges are finished. Seam binding is often used when hemming woolen fabrics.

Here is how to hem a garment with seam binding:

1 Overlap the seam binding about ¼ to ⅜ inch on the right side of the bottom of the garment edge, and stitch with a straight machine stitch.

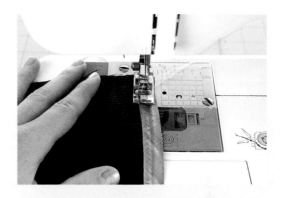

NOTE: If the fabric of the garment tends to fray a great deal, stitch the seam binding on with a zigzag stitch.

2 Fold, press, and pin the hem allowance to the desired width, as previously described. Hand stitch in place with the catch stitch described in "Curved Double-Fold Hems," earlier in this chapter.

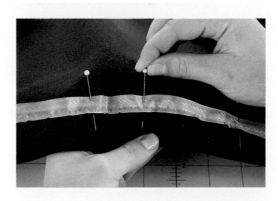

STITCHED AND PINKED HEM

Use the same process as for the stitched-and-pinked edge finish (see Chapter 2). This method works well on fabrics that do not fray too much.

1 Prepare the bottom edge of the garment by straight stitching and then pinking the edge.

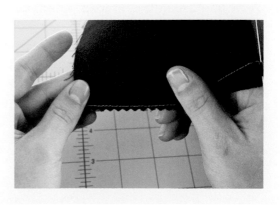

2 Pin up the desired amount of hem allowance and press as previously described.

3 Hand-catch-stitch in place as previously described. Because the edge has been pinked, take your stitch in the hem allowance from the line of straight stitching you made in Step 1.

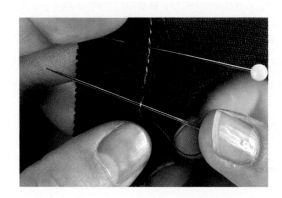

ROLLED OR TINY HEM

Rolled or tiny hems are as narrow as it is physically possible to make them. These hems are usually found on fancy garments made of silk, satin, chiffon, or batiste used in heirloom sewing. There are several ways to make a rolled hem. The hem shown here is finished with a special machine called a serger, but you can also use the zig-zag stitch on a standard machine to make a rolled hem.

While it is possible to use your fingers to roll the hem to the wrong side and stitch with tiny hand stitches, it is easier and faster to use a sewing machine to make the rolled hem.

Your sewing machine may have a presser foot that will do all the work for you as the fabric rolls over through the foot and is then topstitched to make a narrow rolled hem.

If your machine does not have this type of presser foot to roll the hem, you can also use the zigzag stitch to roll the hem of a lightweight fabric such as batiste.

1 Set your sewing machine for a short and wide zigzag with the stitch length set at 0.05 and the stitch width set at 4.

2 Loosen the upper tension slightly. (If you have a foot that has a groove on the bottom, the looser tension will help accommodate the roll.)

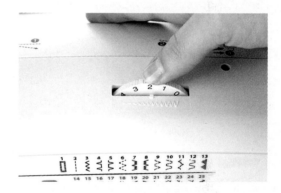

Setting the zigzag

3 Zigzag the raw edge so that the left swing of the zigzag stitch is in the fabric and the right swing of the zigzag stitch is off the edge of the fabric. As the stitch swings back onto the fabric, the thread will pull the edge of the fabric over and roll the edge of the fabric.

FUSED HEM

There are many fusible tapes on the market that altogether eliminate the need for sewing hems. Fusible tape
comes in different widths. It is great if you are in a hurry
and need to hem a garment quickly or do not want any
stitches to show on the right side; however, some tapes
do not stand up to many washings. But if properly fused,
they usually last many years.

4

1 Since you will be fusing with your iron, cut the fusible web tape in lengths about as long as your iron.
A ¼-inch-wide strip of fusible web is usually adequate to fuse a hem. So if the fusible web tape that
you purchased is wider (many come as a ¾-inch tape), cut the web in thirds to make ¼-inch-wide strips
the length of your iron.

2 Place your garment (for which you have measured, pressed up, and prepared the hem as previously
described) on the ironing board wrong side up.

3 Lift the pressed hem allowance and insert the ¼-inch strip of fusible web between the hem allowance and
the garment near the top edge of the hem allowance.

4 Lay a damp press cloth over this section of the hem allowance with the fusible web inside and press
straight down with your steam iron. Hold for 12 to 15 seconds applying pressure. Lift the iron and remove
the press cloth. Let the garment cool slightly before moving it to the next area to be fused. Repeat all
around the hem. Turn the garment over and repeat fusing with the damp press cloth, steaming and applying pressure on the right side.

TIP

Some fabrics, such as napped fabrics—
velvet or corduroy—are not appropriate for
use with fusible tapes.

Fusible tape works best on straight hems
and on fabric that is not too heavy. Read
the packages before you buy, and test the
tape on a scrap of that particular fabric
before you use it on your garment.

Hemline Finishes

Think of a *hemline finish,* adding a decorative or design element to the hemline, as the finishing touch to a garment. Today you are limited only by your comfort level and imagination as to whether or how your hemline is finished. Types of decorative hemline finishes can include trims, laces, sequins, ruffles, flounces, fringes, bands, or a balloon effect, to name just a few.

Hemline with Trim

Some trims have a top-finished edge, while others have a raw unfinished edge. Each would require a different method of application, as explained below.

TRIM WITH A TOP-FINISHED EDGE

Since the top edge is finished, this trim could be topstitched on the right side of the garment hem.

1. On the garment, press a ¼-inch single-fold hem to the outside (right sides together).

2. Pin the trim so that the top edge of the trim covers the raw edge of the hem on the right side (wrong side of trim to right side of garment).

3. Topstitch along the top edge of the trim, catching the raw edge of the turned-up fold in the stitching.

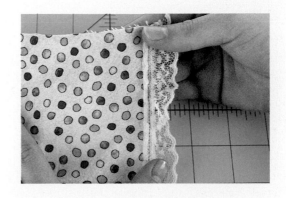

Trim with top-finished edge

FOR TRIM WITH AN UNFINISHED TOP EDGE

If the top edge of the trim is unfinished, it needs to be on the inside of the garment to hide the raw edge.

1. On the garment, press a ¼-inch single-fold hem to the inside (wrong sides together).

2. Pin the trim so that the top edge of the trim covers the raw edge of the hem on the inside (right side of trim to wrong side of garment).

3. Topstitch in place, catching the top of the trim and the pressed-under single fold of the garment.

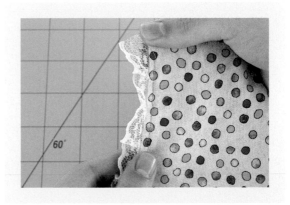

Trim with unfinished top edge

Ruffles

A *ruffle* is a piece of fabric usually cut on the straight grain that can vary in width from less than an inch to many inches. It is gathered on the top and hemmed on the bottom. You can attach it to any garment at the hemline, including pant leg bottoms, sleeve edges, or shoulder edges.

NOTE: Remember that adding a ruffle to the hemline lengthens the garment, so the garment might have to be shortened to get the desired finished length after the ruffle is attached. Ruffles can be made from the garment fabric or from a totally different fabric.

The process of making a ruffle is basically the same for all types of ruffles.

❶ Cut strips of fabric on the straight grain, making them the width you want the ruffle to be, plus seam and hem allowances. A full ruffle is at least 2½ times the length of the edge to which the ruffle will be attached, if it is a fairly lightweight fabric that gathers well. Most ruffles today are less full, at only 1½ times the length of the edge, particularly on a little heavier fabric.

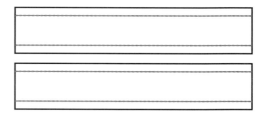

NOTE: These are not precise measurements, only estimates.

❷ Sew the side seams of the ruffle pieces to make one large circle. Press the seams open. Mark the ruffle at the half and quarter points of the circle.

❸ Finish the hem of the ruffle with your preferred method. (Use one of the suggestions given earlier in this chapter.)

Decide how you are going to attach the ruffle to the garment using the suggestions on the following pages. The easiest and most commonly used technique is sewing the right side of the ruffle to the right side of the garment.

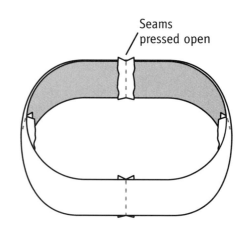

Seams pressed open

RIGHT SIDE OF RUFFLE TO RIGHT SIDE OF GARMENT

1 Either by hand (see Chapter 2, Useful Hand Stitches) or by machine, using the longest stitch length, run one line of basting stitches on top of the ruffle on the seam line.

2 Run a second line of basting stitches in the seam allowance about ¼ inch from the seam line in the seam allowance. Mark the halfway and quarter points of the ruffle.

3 With right sides together, pin one mark to the center front, the next mark to a side seam, the next mark to the center back, and the fourth mark to the other side seam.

4 Gently pull both the gathering threads at the same time so that the gathers are evenly spaced around the garment.

5 Pin the gathering line of the ruffle to the seam line of the garment. The raw edges should be even.

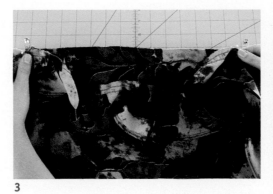

3

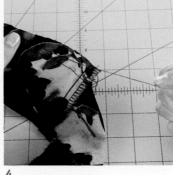

4

6 Sew the ruffle to the garment, sewing directly on top of the basting stitches that were pinned to the seam line. If it is a fabric that might ravel, stitch a second time ¼ inch away in the seam allowance on the second row of basting stitches as a seam finish.

6

WRONG SIDE OF RUFFLE TO RIGHT SIDE OF GARMENT

If you want the top edge of the ruffle to show on the right side of the garment, you need to finish the top edge of the ruffle with a narrow rolled hem (see "Rolled or Tiny Hem," earlier in this chapter). Also, you will need to finish the bottom edge of the garment to prevent fraying. See pages 106–107 for ideas.

1 After you have finished the ruffle's top edge and the garment's bottom edge, stitch one line of basting stitches (for gathering) near the top of the ruffle on the seam line. Mark the halfway and quarter points on the ruffle.

2 Position the wrong side of the ruffle on the right side of the garment hemline, pin one mark to center front, the next mark to a side seam, the next mark to the center back, and the fourth mark to the other side seam. Be sure to have the gathering stitches line up about ½ inch from the bottom edge of the garment.

3 Gently pull the gathering thread so that the gathers are evenly spaced around the garment. Pin in place. On the basting line, topstitch the ruffle to the garment.

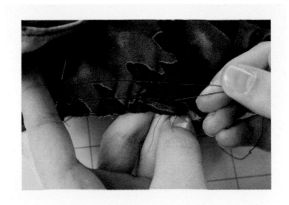

Flounces

A *flounce* is similar to a ruffle except that the top edge of a flounce is exactly the same length as the bottom edge of the garment. A flounce can be any width. The top edge of the flounce is more circular if you want more ripples (fullness) or more elliptical if you want fewer ripples. If you want to make a flounce and your pattern does not include directions for one, follow either of these methods.

METHOD 1

1 Using a flexible tape measure, measure the circumference of the front of the garment hemline by holding the tape measure along the bottom edge of the skirt. Divide this number by 3.

2 On a piece of paper, draw a semi-circle, with the radius being the number you calculated in Step 1.

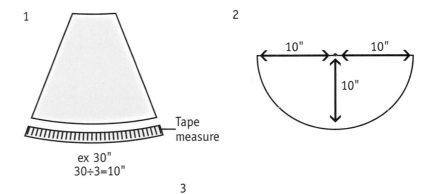

1

Tape measure

ex 30"
30÷3=10"

2

10"   10"

10"

3

3 Determine how wide you want the flounce to be, plus seam allowance and flounce hem (1 inch to 1¼ inches). Using the same center point as in Step 3, draw another semicircle. The radius of this second semicircle is the radius used in Step 1 plus the amount determined earlier, in Step 3 (the total width of the flounce).

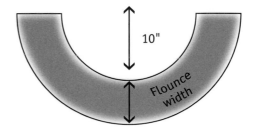

10"

Flounce width

④ Add seam allowances on each end of the semicircle.

4

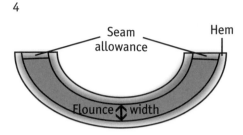

⑤ If the back and front (from seam to seam) are the same, make two flounces the same. If the back and front are different in size, repeat this process for the garment's back flounce.

⑥ Test your flounce pattern pieces by first cutting them out of scrap fabric the same weight as the garment fabric and pinning them to the garment. Make any necessary adjustments to the pattern. When you are satisfied with the flounce, cut the flounce pieces from the garment fabric.

⑦ With right sides together, sew the side seams of the flounce together and hem the flounce using one of the methods described earlier in this chapter.

⑧ With side seams matching and right sides together, pin the front flounce piece to the front of the garment and the back flounce piece to the back of the garment. You may have to ease in the flounce a little. There should not be any gathers. Stitch the flounce to the garment hemline along the seam allowance.

METHOD 2

1 Lay the skirt front of the garment on a piece of paper. Trace the bottom edge of the garment. This is the first arc.

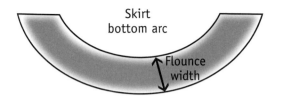

Skirt
bottom arc

Flounce
width

2 Determine how wide you want the flounce to be, plus seam allowance and hem (1 inch to 1¼ inches). With a ruler, mark the arc for a second line at the determined distance (the total width of the flounce). Add a seam allowance on each end of the arc.

3 Connect the marks and cut out the paper pattern.

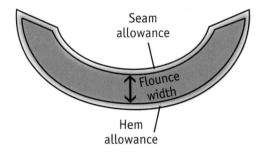

Seam
allowance

Flounce
width

Hem
allowance

4 At approximately evenly spaced points (more for a fuller flounce), cut a straight line from the second arc drawn to the first arc drawn. Do not cut through the first arc.

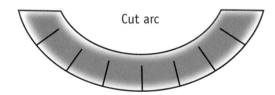

Cut arc

⑤ Evenly spread out the second arc, leaving the first arc line intact. Use more spread for a fuller flounce.

⑥ Retrace the new flounce on another piece of paper and cut it out.

⑦ Follow steps 5–8 from Method 1.

Spread out arc

Bands

To make the skirt two toned, replace a bottom section of the garment with a different fabric, called a band.

Bands can be made from the same fabric as the garment or a contrasting fabric. You can use bands to add length if the garment is too short or simply as a design and decorative element. The finished width of the bands can be whatever width you want or need.

Bands can be narrow and stitched so that they wrap snuggly around the raw edge like a bound edge. This way, they do not add any extra length to the garment and are just a hem finish that is a design element. This type of hem finish is often used on knits.

① To make a narrow band for the hem, cut your band 4 times the width of the desired finished hem. If you are working with a woven fabric, you need to finish one long edge by pressing under ¼ inch and then topstitching. If you are working with a knit fabric, an edge finish is not necessary.

② With right sides together and the raw edges even, stitch the band and garment together with a seam allowance equal to the desired width of the finished band. For example if you wanted a ½-inch finished hem band, cut the material for the band 2 inches wide (½ inch × 4 = 2 inches), and stitch the band onto the garment with a ½-inch seam allowance.

3 Press the band over the seam allowance and snuggly wrap the band around the raw edge of the bottom of the garment so that the raw edge and seam allowance are totally enclosed.

4 Stitch in the ditch from the right side to complete the band. (See Chapter 2 for more on how to stitch in the ditch.)

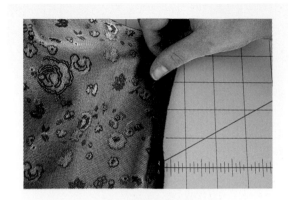

If you are adding a wide band, such as a 2- to 4-inch band that will extend beyond the original length of the garment, you need to shorten the garment accordingly unless you need the extra length. Sewing this extended band around the hemline of a garment is similar to putting on a waistband (see "Waistbands" in Chapter 6).

Balloon

A balloon hemline puffs out at the bottom. They are often found on dressier skirts and dresses. A balloon hemline effect requires a lining that is narrower at the hem edge than the garment. The lining is also shorter than the garment. The narrowness and the shortness of the lining determine how much balloon effect there is on the garment.

1 If you do not have a pattern, make a lining pattern from muslin and pin it to the garment. Adjust the muslin lining by shortening and taking it in at the seams. **Remember:** The smaller and shorter the lining compared to the garment, the more ballooning you have. When you are satisfied with the look, use the muslin as a pattern to cut out the lining.

2 After you sew the side seams of the garment, stitch a basting stitch around the bottom of the garment at the seam allowance. Stitch the seams of the lining together.

3 With right sides together, slip the garment into the lining.

4 At the hem edge, pin the lining and the garment together at all the seams.

3

4

5 Gently gather the garment along the basting line. Pin evenly to the lining.

6 Sew the garment to the lining on the basting stitches.

7 Turn right side out and baste the top edge of the lining to the top edge of the skirt or waistline seam of a dress.

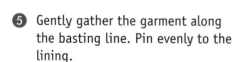

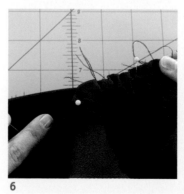

6

7

Raw or Frayed Hem

If a garment has a hem that is on the straight grain (see Chapter 2 for a description of grains) and the fabric is loosely woven, you can easily fray the edge.

NOTE: For an even amount of fringe, the grain must be straight and you need to pull a thread so that the stitching is right on the grain line. If you want to cut off an old pair of blue jeans and leave the hem of each leg uneven and ragged, then that is something different.

① Sew a line of straight or zigzag stitching about 1 inch from the bottom of the garment.

② Pull the horizontal threads away from the vertical threads, or let it happen by itself. If the fabric is tightly woven, just let it be to fray on its own.

TIP

If you snip to the stitching line about every inch, the fraying will go faster and the threads will not get so tangled up.

CHAPTER 6

Waistline Treatments

Over the centuries, garment waistline treatments have varied widely. In the early 1800s, the empire style—a seam line just under the bust rather than a waistline at the natural waist—was in fashion. During the Civil War, women like Scarlett O'Hara—with the aid of someone yanking their corset strings—could constrict their waists to 16 or 18 inches. The 1920s flapper dress had no waistline to speak of; instead, there was a horizontal seam somewhere around the hips. In the 1940s and 1950s, most skirts had a 1- to 2-inch band that encircled a woman's real waist.

In the contemporary fashion world, anything goes in terms of where the waistline of a garment can be and how to "finish" it. Today you decide where you want the top of your skirt to be, even if the pattern calls for something else. You also can choose how to finish the top of your pants, even if the pattern designer had other suggestions.

Waistbands

In earlier decades, skirts and pants had an identifiable waistband. While the waistband varied in width, it was located at the waist; looked like a band; and was fastened with a button, snaps, or hooks and eyes. The waistband's function was not only to finish the top of the skirt or pants, but also to emphasize the narrowness of the waist. Women strove for hourglass figures.

WIDTH

Today, the width of a waistband is not so much to emphasize the narrowness of the waist as it is to be part of the design, while at the same time finishing the top of the skirt or pair of pants. There are no rules for waistbands—whatever suits your fancy, from a mere ½ inch to any number of inches.

You may even prefer to have no waistband at all. (See the "No Waistbands" section, later in this chapter, for instructions for finishing the top of a skirt or pair of pants without a waistband.)

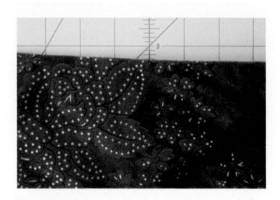

FABRIC

The most obvious waistband fabric is the same fabric you are using for the skirt or pants. However, this doesn't always have to be the case.

For very narrow waistbands and with fabric that isn't bulky, think about trying bias tape, for example.

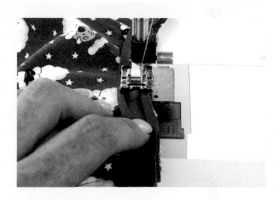

TIP

If you want to add style, try a totally different fabric to add contrast to your garment. If you choose to use different fabrics in the same skirt or pair of pants, try to get fabrics that require the same care. A wide velvet waistband on a cotton skirt might look great, but you will always have to dry-clean the skirt.

FASTENERS

If the skirt or pair of pants has an opening with or without a zipper, you have to decide how the waistband is going to fasten. What you choose for your fastener determines whether you will have overlap, underlap, or no lapping.

| Overlap | Underlap | No lap |

Very narrow waistbands work best with a single hook and eye with very little or no lapping. Wider waistbands work well with one or more buttons or flat waistband hooks and eyes. If the waistband fits you gently, try one or more heavier snaps. It the waistband is going to fit tightly, skip the snaps. You don't want your skirt to come unfastened every time you take a deep breath!

Traditional Waistbands

A traditional waistband is made from the same fabric as the skirt or pants. It is usually between 1 and 2 inches wide and is cut on the straight of grain. It's often one piece of fabric folded in half lengthwise.

1 If you're using a commercial pattern, use the waistband pattern piece or pieces; otherwise, cut a piece of fabric on the straight of grain, 2 to 3 inches longer than your waist and twice the width you want the waistband to be, plus two seam allowances. If you're not using an interfacing, skip to Step 3.

2 If you want a wide waistband or your fabric is softly woven, consider using interfacing to stiffen it up. Fold the waistband in half lengthwise and press it if you are using a one-piece foldover band. The interfacing should come just up to the fold on the wrong side of one half of the waistband. Press the interfacing onto the wrong side of the lower half of the waistband. If you have softer fabric, use a lightweight iron-on interfacing and cover the whole wrong side of the waistband.

3 Fold the waistband in half lengthwise, with the wrong sides together, and press. Press the seam allowance to the inside on one edge of the waistband without the notches.

4 Now turn the waistband so the right sides are together, but do not crease. Sew the ends of the waistband together. Trim the corners, then turn the waistband right side out and press the corners.

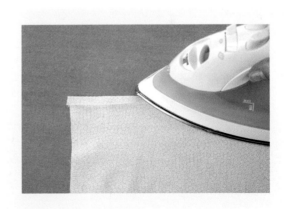

5 With the right sides together and matching notches, pin the unfolded edge (refer to Step 3)—*the notched edge*—of the waistband to the top of the skirt or pants. Adjust as needed. Depending on how you have chosen to finish the closing, the ends of the waistband will extend beyond the skirt/pants edge. You will use these ends for the underlap and overlap where you will place buttons, snaps, or hooks and eyes.

6 Sew the notched edge of the waistband to the skirt or pants and press the seam allowances toward the waistband. Fold the pressed-up seam allowance edge to the wrong side of the garment.

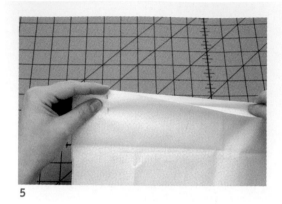

5

7 Beginning in the middle of the waistband, pin the folded edge of the waistband to the wrong side of the skirt or pants, placing the pins as described for the stitch-in-the-ditch seam (see Chapter 2).

You will be pinning from the right side and catching the fold of the back side of the waistband. Be sure the heads of the pins are toward you when you sew. This will make them easier to remove as you sew.

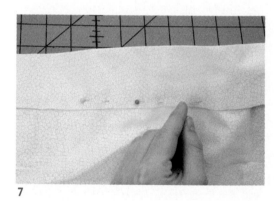

7

8 Sew in the ditch from the right side, removing pins as you go.

9 When you come to the overlap and underlap, top-stitch to the end of the waistband. You may prefer to hand-slip-stitch the openings closed. The photo shows the finished product.

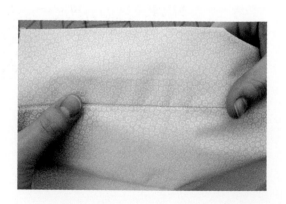

Waistbands with Ties

Wraparound skirts often have long ties instead of underlaps or overlaps. (See Chapter 7 for more on wraparound skirts.) Some pants also have ties, as do aprons.

1 Make a long tie using either method described in the section on ties, straps, and belts in Chapter 2. Instead of sewing the whole length of the tie, leave the center of the tie unsewn the length of the waistline of the skirt. Turn the tie right side out if necessary.

2 Follow the steps for attaching a waistband to a skirt or pants in the previous section and attach the open center of the tie as if it were a traditional waistband.

FAQ

How long do I make the ties?

The length of the tie depends on how you're going to tie it. For example, if you plan to make a bow or you want the ends of the tie to reach the hemline, you will need a longer tie. If you want just a square knot, shorter tie ends will be OK.

Double-Fold Bias Tape Waistbands

Using double-fold bias tape is a quick and easy way to finish a skirt or pair of pants. The bias in the tape fits smoothly to any curve of the waistline. It's also sewn just one time around the top of the pants or skirt. Double-fold bias tape has one side that's slightly narrower than the other side, which makes it possible to sew close to the edge of the narrow side and catch the wider side in the stitching on the wrong side (inside).

① Select the ½-inch or 1-inch double-fold bias tape in either a matching or contrasting color to the skirt or pants. See page 161 in Chapter 7 on how to apply bias tape to not distort the ⅝ inch seam allowance.

② Slip the bias tape over the edge of the skirt with the narrower side to the outside and the wider side to the inside.

2

③ Pin the tape in place.

④ Decide how you're going to finish the ends. You might find it easier to leave the ends unsewn and slip-stitch them by hand later. If there is a great deal of bulk, the machine needle sometimes slips off the edge of the bias tape.

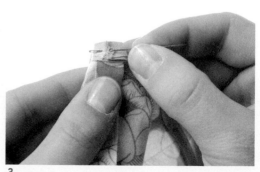

3

⑤ From the right side, topstitch the tape in place. **Remember:** Your stitches will show, so choose your thread accordingly. If you have pinned properly, the stitches will catch the bias tape on the underside.

⑥ Finish the ends.

5

If your garment is made of a lightweight to medium-weight fabric and has a zipper in the back seam, finish the ends with no overlap or underlap. Use one or more hooks and eyes to finish off the top of the zipper.

FAQ

How Do I Make My Own Bias Tape?

1. Decide how wide you want the finished tape to be and multiply that width by 4. This measurement is an approximation of the width of the bias strips you will need to cut.

2. Cut your fabric straight across from selvage to selvage. Then fold the cut edge diagonally so that it matches the selvage. Cut on this folded line. Using this cut (on the bias) as the starting point, cut several strips the width you need.

3. Stitch the ends of the strips together.

4. Press the strip not quite in half lengthwise. Carefully fold the lengthwise edges to the center and press. Try not to burn your fingers with the hot iron.

No Waistbands

You can make a skirt or a pair of pants with no waistband—especially if the top of the skirt or pants sits on your hips and not at your waist—by using a lining, facing, or yoke to finish the waistline edge.

Lining

The easiest way to finish the top of a skirt if you're not using a traditional waistband is to add a lining. The lining is basically the same size as the skirt.

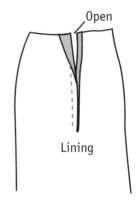

Open

Lining

1. Sew all seams of the garment and put in the zipper (if you want one). Sew all the seams of the lining, leaving the zipper opening open. (For more on zippers, see Chapter 2.)

NOTE: With this method, you don't have to finish the seams unless your fabric frays easily.

2. With right sides together, matching seams and notches, sew the garment to the lining around the top edge with a ⅝-inch seam.

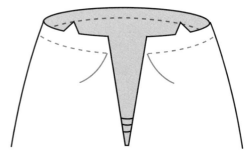

Right sides together

③ Grade the seam and clip the curve if necessary.

④ Press the seam allowance toward the lining and understitch the lining to both seam allowances. (For how to understitch, see Chapter 2.)

NOTE: For more on how to grade seams and clip curves, see Chapter 2.

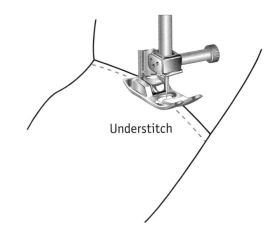

Understitch

⑤ Turn the garment right side out and press seam flat. Finish the opening around the zipper by turning under the seam allowance on the lining and hand-stitching the lining to the zipper tape. Finish the top of the zipper opening with hook and eye if needed.

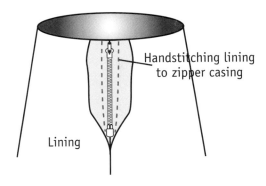

Handstitching lining to zipper casing

Lining

FAQ

Is the process for putting in a facing different from the process for putting in a lining?

The process of putting in a facing is exactly the same as putting in a lining, except that the facing is much shorter in length.

1. After the facing seams have been sewn together, finish the facing hem.
2. Follow the steps on this and the previous page for putting in a lining.

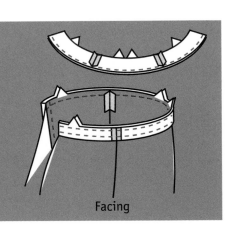

Facing

Casings

If you plan to put elastic at the top of a skirt or pair of pants, follow any of the methods below; just put the elastic in before you finish the ends of the casing. Firmly attach the elastic to the garment at both ends. (For more on casings, see Chapter 2.)

1. In addition to the methods described in Chapter 2, you can create a casing by stitching the bottom and top folds of single-fold bias tape to the wrong side of the garment at the waistline.

1

2. If the elastic is narrow and you have a large enough seam allowance, make a double-fold hem at the top of the garment for the elastic. Insert the elastic in the casing and stitch the two ends together as described in Chapter 2.

3. If you plan to have a drawstring, make a buttonhole in the center front before you finish sewing the casing down.

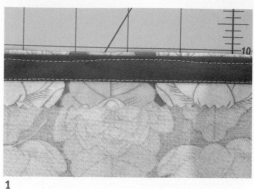

2

If you have a full skirt and you don't want darts or a narrow waistband casing with elastic, try shirring the waistband. Shirring is characterized by several horizontal lines, usually of very thin or narrow elastic that gathers the fabric. If the shirring doesn't need to stretch, string is used instead of elastic. There are several ways to make a shirring waist finish and three ways are presented below.

1 Use regular thread in the needle and elastic in the bobbin. Sew several rows of stitching about ¼ inch apart in the waistband if there is one, or at the top of the skirt or pants if there is no waistband. If you plan to add shirring and there is no waistband, add 2 or more inches to the top of the skirt/pant pieces. Although the shirring can be made as a separate waistband and then attached to the skirt or pants, it is usually made as an extension of the garment.

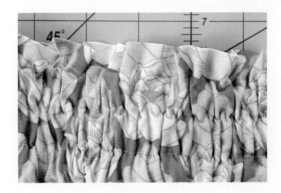

2 Make several parallel casings with ½-inch bias tape. Thread the elastic through each casing.

3 In a wide traditional waistband, sew several parallel lines of stitching. Thread the elastic through the "tunnels."

CHAPTER 7

Necklines, Armholes, and Straps

One of the first parts of a garment people notice is the neckline. As with hemlines and waists, necklines have varied from the ruffs of the Elizabethan age to the deeply plunging necklines of the past few decades. Some necklines have collars and some have facings, piping, or other trim. Coupled with the neckline treatment are the sleeves. On some garments, such as sleeveless tops or raglan sleeves, the neckline and the sleeve/armhole are considered together. Sleeves vary in size, style, fullness, and length—they come as full and puffy as Princess Diana's wedding dress or as thin as angel hair spaghetti. As with all other aspects of fashion design, the choices are limitless and entirely up to you, the creator.

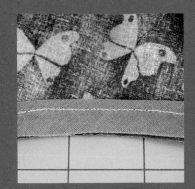

Necklines

Despite the myriad of necklines that have existed in women's fashion throughout the centuries, there are really only a few basic shapes. Remember that the front and back necklines don't have to be the same.

Neckline Shapes

The **boatneck** opening is one of the easiest necklines to make. (See Chapter 10 for instructions on how to make a boatneck top.) This neckline is a horizontal line on both the back and front. The back and front shoulder seams are sewn together, leaving the middle of the seam open wide enough for your head. The opening is finished as a hem (see Chapter 5).

The **round neck** opening is cut in an approximate circle with the front neckline a little lower than the back to fit the shape of your neck. The edge of the neckhole touches the neck in the front and back. Because the neckhole is usually smaller in diameter than the head, a slit is made in either the center of the front or back seam or in the shoulder seams. Often these neckholes are finished with a facing, but there are several other ways to finish a round neckline. See suggestions for finishing necklines later in this chapter.

The **scoop neck** is similar to a round neck opening except that the circle is larger. The amount of scoop is up to you as the designer. You may want to mix and match, using a scoop neck in the front or back and a round neck on the other side. If the scoop is large enough to fit over the head, there is no need for another opening. If the scoop is not large enough, an opening is inserted in the center front or back. Often these necklines are finished with a facing, but there are several other ways to finish a scoop neckline. See suggestions for finishing necklines later in this chapter.

The **square neck** can be any size and can be in the front and/or the back. It usually requires a facing to ensure perfectly neat corners. See "Facings" later in this chapter.

The **V-neck** can be any depth, with the V pointing to the center of the front and/or the back. The easiest method for finishing a V-neck is with a facing to ensure a perfect V shape. See "Facings" later in this chapter.

Collars

To the basic shape of the neck opening, various collars can be attached. Collars and their shapes change as fashions change. Because there are so many types, styles, and sizes of collars, I can describe only a few of the more basic ones. Follow your pattern for more directions on specific collars and how they are attached to the garment.

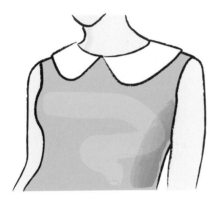  

Flat collars, such as the Peter Pan collar, lie flat on the shoulders and on the back and front because the collar is shaped. They can be made in one or two pieces. These collars should be interfaced and sewn very accurately to keep shape and symmetry. See "Interfacing" later in this chapter. They can also be made independent of the garment and worn on top of any round-neck sweater or blouse.

Rolled collars have little shaping at the neck edge. This lack of shaping causes the collar to roll. The place where the collar naturally wants to roll is called the *roll line*. This effect can be enhanced by cutting the upper collar slightly larger than the under collar. The *upper collar* is what is seen by the public. The *under collar* is on the underside of the upper collar and not usually seen unless one wears the collar straight up and not resting on the shoulders and back.

Stand-up collars include turtlenecks, mandarin collars, and band collars. These collars are cut as rectangles and sewn to the neck edge.

See "Facings" later in this chapter for more information on attaching a collar to the top.

Sleeves also come in a variety of shapes and sizes, from "leg-of-mutton" to no sleeve at all. Sleeves carry names, such as raglan, drop, set-in, long, short, caplets, or three-quarters. They can be embellished with or without cuffs, buttons, or other trims, ruffles, or laces.

  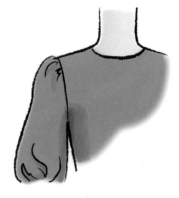

A **set-in sleeve** can be any length. Its identifying characteristic is that there are no gathers or tucks at the top of the sleeve where it is sewn into the armhole. For instructions on how to make a set-in sleeve, see "Make Set-In Sleeves" later in this chapter.

Raglan sleeves can be any length and have no armhole seam, but rather a diagonal line from the underarm to the neckline. They are often found in jackets, coats, and sweatshirts, but also in dresses and blouses. Because of the shape of the sleeve, the top of the sleeve is part of the neckline.

The **gathered or puffy sleeve** can be any length and is cut wider at the top than a set-in sleeve. In contrast to the set-in sleeve, the top of a puffy sleeve (where it attaches to the armhole) is gathered or pleated, creating a puffy look.

Drop sleeves do not have armhole seams. The sleeves are cut as part of the front and back pieces.

Sleeveless tops have armholes that are finished with binding, trim, or facings. See "Facings" later in this chapter for more information on how to finish armholes.

TIP

When inserting sleeves in a garment that will experience a great deal of wear, sew a piece of bias tape about 4 inches long into the underarm seam allowance before or after sewing the sleeve to the garment.

Make Set-in Sleeves

Of the sleeve types just mentioned, set-in sleeves are the most difficult to get right. The goal with set-in sleeves is to not have any tucks, pleats, or wrinkles in the armhole seam on either the garment or the sleeve. Achieving this goal is a little tricky because you're sewing a relatively sharp curve, the top of the sleeve, to a relatively straight edge, the garment armhole. The stiffer the fabric, the more difficult it is. Every sewing expert has a magic way to do it. My method is "You can't use too many pins!"

① Mark the dot on the top of the sleeve clearly. Also, single-notch the front of the sleeve and front of the garment and double-notch the back of the sleeve and back of the garment.

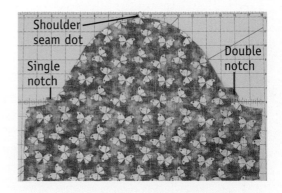

Shoulder seam dot

Double notch

Single notch

② On the sleeve, machine-baste a running stitch using a longer stitch length along the seam line between the notches. For more on uses for running stitches, see Chapter 2.

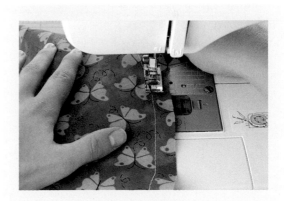

3 Very gently slide the fabric along the gathering stitches. This is not a big gather as for a ruffle, but a very minor ease so that the sleeve will fit smoothly inside the armhole.

NOTE: If possible, sew the sleeves in before you sew the underarm seam of the sleeves or garment.

4 With right sides together and notches matching, pin the sleeve to the garment such that the sleeve is on top. You will be stitching on top of the gathering thread. Start pinning from the underarm seam to the notches.

5 Pin the dot on the top of sleeve to the shoulder seam.

6 Using as many pins as necessary, pin the ease of the sleeve to the armhole. Keep adjusting the gathering until it fits perfectly. Be patient.

7 When you think that you have the sleeve pinned to the garment enough, put the speed of your sewing machine as slow as it will go and very carefully begin stitching from the underarm seam, pulling the pins just before you get to them so that you don't accidentally hit a pin and dull your machine needle. Remember, the sleeve is on top as you stitch.

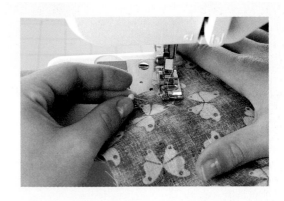

8 When you get to the notch marking the beginning of the ease, sew directly on top of the gathering stitches.

9 Since the armhole can be a stress point, double stitch it for added strength by stitching a second row of stitching about ⅛ inch inside the seam on the seam allowance. Trim the lower curve of the armhole below the notches to a ¼-inch seam allowance.

Facings

Facings are used to finish edges at necklines, armholes, and front or back openings. The edge of the facing that is attached to the garment is cut to match the edge to be faced. If the garment fabric is light to medium weight, the facings are cut from the same fabric. If the fabric is heavyweight, the facing is made from a lightweight or lining fabric.

Basic Neck Facing

If you have a pattern, follow the directions for making the facing. If you don't have a pattern and want to make a facing, follow these steps. It doesn't matter what shape the neckline is—round, scoop, square, or V—the basic process is the same.

❶ On a piece of paper, trace the garment neckline. Don't forget to add the seam allowance at the shoulders and opening if the garment is already stitched.

If, instead of a pattern, you have the garment in pieces, trace each piece separately.

❷ Repeat the shape of the neckline about 2–3 inches from the neckline edge.

1

❸ Cut out the facing pattern pieces. Using these pattern pieces, cut out the facings from the fabric.

❹ If you are not using interfacing, skip to Step 5. If you're using interfacing, press the interfacing onto the facing (see "Interfacing" later in this chapter).

3

⑤ If there are no shoulder seams on the facing, skip to Step 6. If there are shoulder seams on the facing, sew them together and press them open.

⑥ Finish the bottom edge of the facing. Choose an option (a hem or seam finish) with very little bulk (see chapters 5 and 2 for more on hem and seam finishes).

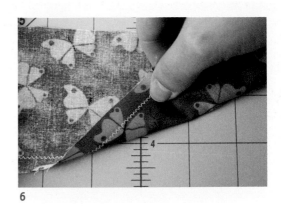

6

⑦ With right sides of garment and facing together, match the shoulder seams and the front and back center points and stitch the facing to the neckline with a ⅝ inch seam.

⑧ Press the seam allowance toward the facing. Grade the seam, clip, and under-stitch. See Chapter 2 for more on under-stitching.

⑨ Press the facing to the inside of the garment.

7

⑩ Hand-slip-stitch the facing to the garment at the shoulder seams. See Chapter 2 for hand stitches.

⑪ Finish any neck openings, such as a zipper. Fold under the ends of the facing seam allowance and slip-stitch the folds in place—for example, to the zipper tape.

10

Basic Armhole Facing

Prepare armhole facings in the same way as neckline facings, with a few exceptions.

1 The armhole front and back facing are usually cut as one piece so that the facing has only one seam at the underarm and no shoulder seam.

2 It's important to make a left and a right armhole facing. The front curve and the back curve of the armhole are not necessarily the same. Mark the front and back and the left facing and right facing so you won't get confused.

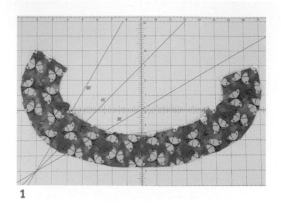

1

3 Interface (optional) and finish the outer edge of each facing. (See Chapter 2.)

4 If you have already sewn the side seams of the garment, sew the underarm seams of the facing together. With right sides together, match the facing underarm seam with garment underarm seam and the top of facing with the shoulder seam. Pin and stitch the facing to the garment. If you haven't sewn the underarm seam together, do not sew the underarm seam of the facing. Sew the facing to the garment first. Then finish the underarm seam of the garment and facing.

4

5 Press the seam allowance toward the facing. Grade the seam, clip the curve, and under-stitch (See Chapter 2).

6 Press the facing to the inside of the garment.

7 Hand-slip-stitch the facing to the garment at the shoulder and underarm seams. See Chapter 2 for hand stitching.

5

One-Piece Neck and Armhole Facing

Some tank tops and sleeveless dresses have one facing that finishes the neckline and armholes at the same time. This facing eliminates bulk at the shoulders where separate neckline and armhole facings would overlap. You have to put this facing on before you sew the shoulder seams of the garment and facing or you won't be able to turn the facing to the inside.

If you don't have a pattern and want to make a facing, follow these steps:

1 On a sheet of paper, trace the neckline and armhole lines, adding seam allowance where needed.

2 Follow the basic curve of the neckline and make a second line 2–3 inches below the first. Repeat with the armholes.

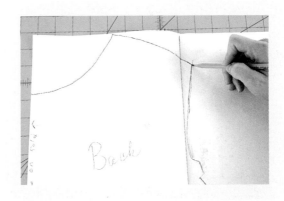

③ Smooth out the bottom line where the neck and armhole line meet. Cut out the pattern.

④ Interface (optional). See the suggestions on page 159 later in this chapter. If you choose not to interface, skip to Step 5.

⑤ Finish the bottom edge of the facing. Choose the least bulky finish (see the chapters on hem or seam finishes).

⑥ Sew the side seams of the garment together. Repeat with the facing side seams.

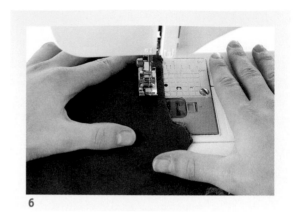

6

⑦ With right sides together, match the front and back center points and the side seams. Pin.

⑧ Stitch the armholes and neckline edges together. Do not sew the shoulder seams together.

⑨ Press the seam allowance toward the facing. Grade the seam, clip the curve, and under-stitch where possible. See Chapter 2.

⑩ Turn the facing and garment right side out.

⑪ Carefully stitch the shoulder seams of the garment together without getting the facing caught in the seam. Press the seams open.

11

TIP

Cut the facing $\frac{1}{16}$ inch smaller at the armhole and necklines so that the seams will roll to the inside slightly and not show from the right side of the garment.

⑫ Press the facing seam allowances to the inside.

12

⑬ Pin the ends under on the facing seam.

13

⑭ Press the facing seam allowances to the inside and hand-slip-stitch the shoulder seam of the facing closed. See Chapter 2 for hand-slip-stitching.

14

Facing with a Collar

Here are the basic directions for putting in a collar:

1 Make the collar and prepare the facing according to your purchased pattern or steps 1–9 under "Basic Neck Facing" above.

2 Baste the collar in place on the garment, matching the notches. The right side of the under-collar will be to the right side of the garment.

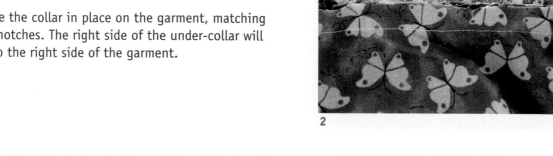

2

3 Pin and sew the facing to the neckline with the collar between the facing and the garment. There will be several layers of fabric in the seam. It is important to grade this seam to eliminate some of the bulk. Finish as previously described with other neckline facings.

3

Interfacing

Interfacing is used to stiffen up certain parts of a garment—for example, a waistband, buttonhole band, a facing, a cuff, or a collar. Interfacing also helps the fashion fabric lie flat. As its name implies, interfacing goes between two layers of fabric such as between the facing and the garment or between collar, cuff, or waistband pieces that need some extra body for support or to lie flat. There are many different brands of interfacing on the market, and they are constantly being updated and changed. Go to several fabric stores to find out what is available.

There are several kinds of interfacing to choose from: woven or nonwoven and fusible (ironed on) or nonfusible (sewn on). *Woven interfacings* include Organdy, Lawn, Batiste, and Organza. *Nonwoven interfacings* include a variety of weights of fusible and sew-in fabrics. *Fusible interfacing* is becoming the preference of most home sewers (see below). Interfacing also comes in a wide variety of weights and several neutral colors.

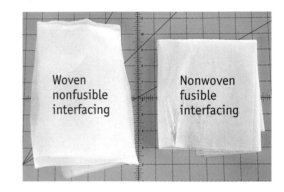

Woven
nonfusible
interfacing

Nonwoven
fusible
interfacing

Nonfusible or *sew-in interfacing* is used on lightweight, sheer, or see-through fabric, because the glue of the fusible might show through. Non-woven interfacing is used for most home sewing and general sewing. Woven interfacing is used for tailoring.

Your pattern will suggest how much and what kind will work with their suggested fabrics. A general rule is to choose an interfacing that is slightly lighter in weight than the fabric. Always do a test sample of the fabric and interfacing to 'feel' if that weight and type of interfacing gives the desired results for that particular garment area and fabric.

FAQ

When and how do I use fusible interfacing?

Fusible interfacing is easy to use and is suitable for most applications and fabrics. Textured fabrics such as seersucker or napped fabrics are not suitable for use with fusible interfacing. All the bumps or nap get flattened and disappear. Fabrics that are sensitive to heat or have been waterproofed also do not take fusible interfacing. Always do a small test fusing on a scrap piece of your garment fabric to make sure it can be successfully fused.

Some fusible interfacings require steam, and others do not. When you press the fusible to the fabric, do not push the iron back and forth. Place the iron on the fusible interfacing, count the number of seconds suggested by the manufacturer, lift the iron, and place it in a different location.

Other Finishes for Necklines and Armholes

If you do not want to finish the neckline and/or sleeveless armholes with a facing, you can use either single or double fold bias tape, or some other form of trim.

SINGLE FOLD BIAS TAPE

1 Sew a stay-stitch around the neckline/armhole, just barely to the seam allowance side of the sewing line.

2 Clip to but not through the stay-stiching in several places (evenly spaced) around the edge.

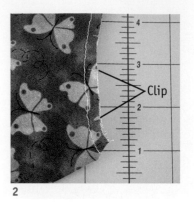

3 Open one edge of bias tape and pin the crease on the stay-stitches with the right side of the tape to the right side of the garment.

4 Stitch on the crease to sew the tape to the garment.

5 Press the bias tape to the inside along the seam line (see photo). Try to keep the bias tape from showing on the public/right side of the garment.

6 Carefully hand-slip-stitch the bias tape to the inside of the garment. Or topstitch the bias tape to the garment along the bottom crease of the bias tape.

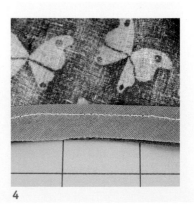

DOUBLE FOLD BIAS TAPE

1. Choose a color of bias tape that matches or compliments your garment.

2. Sew a stay-stitch around the neckline/armhole, just barely to the seam allowance side of the sewing line.

3. Trim close to the stay-stitching, being careful not to cut the stay-stitches (see photo).

3

4. Slip the bias tape over the garment's raw edge with the narrower edge of the bias tape to the right side of the garment just barely covering stay-stitching and the wider edge of the bias tape to the inside of the garment. Pin, then topstitch the bias tape in place through all thicknesses.

4

TIP

Other trims and laces

Follow the directions for finishing a hem with trim or lace in Chapter 5. Prepare the neckline/armhole with one of the methods described above. Begin at the back seam for necklines and underarm seam for armholes to sew on the lace or trim.

Straps

Most straps, regardless of width, are made in one of two ways: fold and sew or sew and turn. See Chapter 2 for basic directions for these two methods. Straps typically connect the back and front of a garment. A variation is the halter top, which goes from front to front around the back of the neck and is usually tied in the back of the neck.

Strap Closures and Attachments

Straps can be sewn in place on both ends—front and back—or sewn into the garment at one end and attached in a variety of ways on the other end. Having one end that attaches with a button or snap makes it easier to get in and out of the garment.

BUTTON WITH OR WITHOUT BUTTONHOLES

There are so many different buttons today that it's fun to just look at them. Buttons can be decorative, functional, or both. If you want to use a button and buttonhole on your straps, you have a few options.

DESIGN 1

1. Finish the end of the strap where the buttonhole will go with a V or round end. See Chapter 2 for making straps. After the strap is made, put the buttonhole on the finished end of the strap. Adjust the length of the strap at the sewn-in unfinished end.

2. Sew the button in place on the garment after the facing is in.

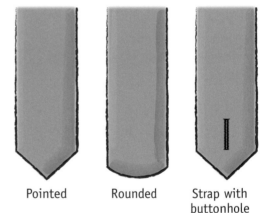

Pointed   Rounded   Strap with buttonhole

DESIGN 2

If you don't want a buttonhole but still want a button for decorative purposes, finish the end of the strap where the button will go with a V or rounded end. Sew the button on the right side of the end of the strap. Attach a snap or hook-and-loop tape to the underside of the strap and right side of the garment. One advantage to this method is that you can adjust the length of the strap by moving the snap.

Strap Embellishments

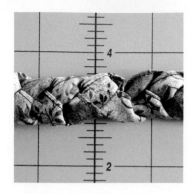
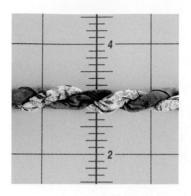
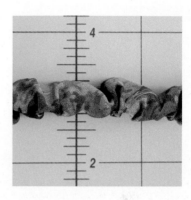

BRAID

1. Make three straps using one of the methods suggested in Chapter 2. Make the straps several inches longer than you need and approximately ¼ inch–½ inch wide.

2. Sew the ends of the three straps together at one end and then braid the straps together. Continue braiding until the braid is the length you need.

3. Fasten the unsewn end of the braid with a few machine or hand stitches.

4. Baste the ends of the braided strap in place before you put on the facing, unless otherwise directed by your pattern.

TWIST

1. Make two or more straps using one of the methods suggested in Chapter 2. Make the straps several inches longer than you need and ½–1 inch wide.

2. Sew one end of the straps together and then twist the straps together. Continue twisting until the twist is the length you need; it can be as tight or as loose as you want.

3. Fasten the end of the twist with a few stitches.

4. Baste the ends of the twisted strap in place right sides together before you put on the facing, unless otherwise directed by your pattern.

ELASTIC

1. Make the straps several inches longer than needed using one of the methods suggested in Chapter 2.

2. Measure the elastic to the length required for the desired finished length of the strap plus 1 inch for seam allowances.

3. Thread the elastic through the straps. Stitch the elastic to the straps at both ends.

4. Baste the ends of the elastic strap in place with the right side to the right side of the garment before you put on the facing, unless otherwise directed by your pattern.

CHAPTER 8

Skirts

Over the years and centuries, skirts have experienced an infinite number of changes. Hemlines go up, hemlines go down. Hemlines are straight, hemlines are not straight. Some of the names for various lengths and styles of skirts have also changed. Do not let that worry you. Today, anything goes, regardless of what you call it, as long as it flatters your body shape and fits your lifestyle.

Skirt Lengths and Shapes

In spite of all the variations in style, the two important measurements to keep in mind when making a skirt are your waist and hip circumference. In addition, you need to know how long and how full you want the skirt to be beyond the basic wearing ease of 2 to 4 inches.

SKIRT LENGTHS

Once you master the basic techniques of waists, hems, and closures, you are ready to make any number of different skirts. Some of the different skirt lengths are listed below, from the shortest to the longest.

- **Micromini:** The waistline has often been lowered and the hemline has been raised to what society and modesty allow.

- **Mini:** The hemline is somewhere mid-thigh.

- **Knee:** The hemline is at the knee, slightly above, or slightly below.

- **Midi:** The hemline is just below the knee around mid-calf.

- **Ballerina/tea:** The hemline is below mid-calf and above the ankle.

- **Ankle:** The hemline is at the ankle.

- **Floor:** The hemline is slightly above the floor.

SKIRT SHAPES AND STYLES

The skirt you design and create can be any combination of length, style, and shape. The following are general descriptions of common skirt designs. There is no limit to variation within each style.

- **Straight:** All the vertical seam lines in a straight skirt are perpendicular to the floor. The width at the hem is approximately the same as the width at the hip. A pencil skirt is a variation of the straight skirt; it is tighter fitting

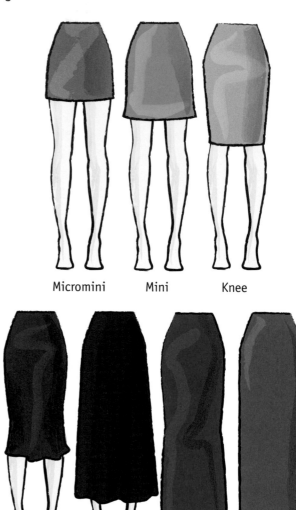

Micromini   Mini   Knee

Midi   Ballerina/tea   Ankle   Floor

and has a slight indention in the side seams below the hips to accentuate the body shape, causing the hem to be narrower than the hip measurement. A pencil skirt is often short with the hem at or slightly below the knee.

- **A-line:** The waist is the narrowest part of the skirt, which gradually becomes wider toward the hem.

- **Flared:** Similar in shape to an A-line skirt, except it is much wider at the hemline and it may be fitted or gathered at the waist.

- **Gored:** Gores are the pieces in a skirt. An eight-gore skirt, for example, has eight vertical pieces and eight vertical seams.

- **Tiered:** A skirt created by sewing several horizontal gathered strips of fabric, one on the bottom of the next. One skirt can contain any number of strips of different fabrics, or tier widths. The more tiers and gathers, the wider the skirt at the hem.

- **Balloon:** The hem of a balloon skirt is attached to a shorter and narrower lining, causing the skirt fabric to balloon out at the hem.

- **Circle:** A circle skirt is just that: a circle at the waistline and at the hemline. There are no tucks, gathers, or pleats at the waist because the waistline is a circle with the circumference equal to the wearer's waist.

- **Wraparound:** A wraparound skirt can be straight, A-line, or flared. The front or back is extended to wrap around and overlap on the front or the back.

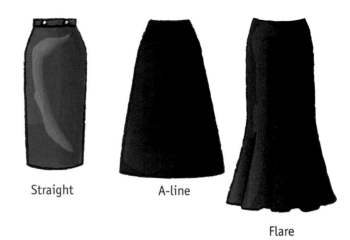

Straight   A-line

Flare

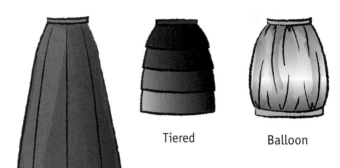

Tiered   Balloon

Gored

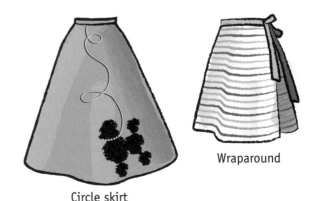

Circle skirt   Wraparound

Design Your Own Skirt Patterns

Designing your own skirt patterns is simple, once you have practiced the basics. Pull-on, straight, A-line, and wrap skirts are the easiest of all skirt patterns to create.

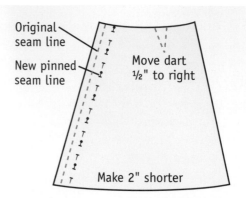

Original seam line

New pinned seam line

Move dart ½" to right

Make 2" shorter

Materials

To design your own skirt patterns, you will need:

- A large sheet of paper. Try to find newsprint with 1-inch squares; most office supply stores sell it.

- Tape measure.

- A yardstick.

- Your waist (W) and hip (H) measurements.

- The finished length (L) you want the skirt to be.

NOTE: You can skip the next steps and just trace the pieces of one of your favorite skirts as a starting point. Do not forget to add the seam allowances (see chapters 2 and 3).

Pull-On Skirt Pattern

This skirt is so simple that you could probably skip making a pattern and start cutting right away as long as your fabric was folded double on the lengthwise grain. To be on the safe side, try a muslin mock-up first. See Chapter 4 for information on making a muslin mock-up.

1 Make one rectangle of the paper pattern with the length of the rectangle equal to the length you want the skirt to be plus hem allowance plus 1½ inches for elastic waist casing.

2 The width of the rectangle is half your hip measurement plus 2 to 6 inches of ease plus seam allowance. The standard seam allowance is ⅝ inch.

Directions for putting this skirt together can be found later in this chapter in the section "Pull–On Skirt."

Straight Skirt Pattern

FRONT PATTERN PIECE

① On a long, straight edge of the paper (this edge of the pattern will be placed on the fold), place a mark a few inches down from the top of the paper and mark this point (T). From (T), measure down L inches (the length you want the skirt to be plus the hem allowance and waist seam allowance). Mark this point (L). The seam allowance can be ⅝ or ½ inch. Be consistent in each garment. See Step 11.

Length of skirt

T

L

1

② At both (T) and at (L), draw a line perpendicular to the fold (edge of the paper). The T–L line of the pattern will be placed on the fold of the fabric (center front).

T

Center front

Place on fold

L

2

③ At (T), measure up the edge of the paper about ½ inch and place another line perpendicular to the edge/fold line. Place a mark (B) on this line that is equal to one-quarter of your waist measurement plus seam allowance plus ease (2 to 4 inches).

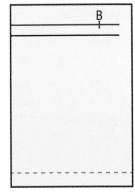

B

T

L

3

④ From T to B, draw a slightly upward curved line. The curved line should intersect T at right angles. This will be your waistline curve or the top of the skirt.

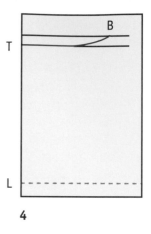

4

⑤ Decide where your hip line is (the fullest part of your hip). It is probably about 4 to 8 inches (HL) below your waistline.

⑥ Draw another line perpendicular to the edge of the paper HL inches below (T) or your waistline point. Starting from the edge of the paper, mark a point on this line, about one-quarter of your hip measurement plus seam allowance plus ease (2 to 4 inches). Mark this point C.

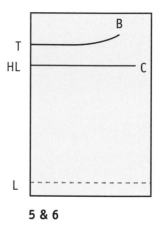

5 & 6

⑦ Draw a slightly curved line from B to C. This line will correspond to your shape down your side from the waist to the hip.

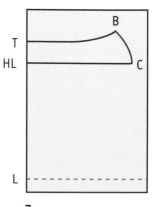

7

8 Draw a line parallel to the edge of the paper from C to line L. This will be the rest of the side seam.

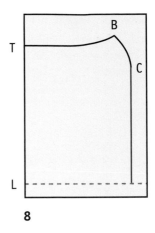

8

9 To draw the hemline, measure the length with your yardstick from the T-B curved waistline, making dots along L in several places. (The dots will leave line L and begin to follow the curve of the waistline.) Connect the dots; the hem will curve slightly up at the side seam line.

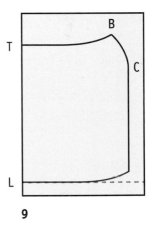

9

10 Label the top and bottom of your pattern piece to indicate the top as the waist and the bottom as the hem. Cut out the pattern piece. This will be the front pattern piece.

10

BACK PATTERN PIECE

⑪ Make another pattern piece by tracing the front piece, but instead of placing the T–L line on the edge of the paper, place the T–L line a seam allowance away from the edge (for the back seam). The seam allowance, again, is ⅝ or ½ inch. Choose one and be consistent for each garment.

⑫ After making a muslin skirt from your pattern (see Chapter 4), check the fit and adjust the pattern accordingly. You may need to make derriere or tummy darts.

Directions for making this skirt follow later in this chapter, in the "Basic Straight Skirt" section.

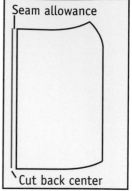

Seam allowance

Cut back center

11

A-Line Skirt Pattern

1–6 Follow steps 1–6 for the straight skirt, except in Step 3 measure up between ½ inch and 1 inch and place a line perpendicular to the edge (B).

7 Using a yardstick, connect point B to point C and continue the line to L, which is the desired length plus hem and waist seam allowance.

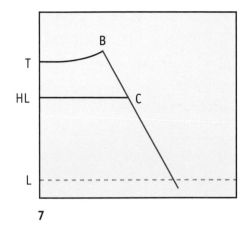

7

8 Using your yardstick and starting at the center front, mark the hem L inches from the waistline curve. The distance from the waistline to the hemline should be the same from the center front to the side seam.

This will be the front piece. If you plan to have just side seams, the back pattern piece will be the same as the front pattern piece, except make the waistline curve a little shallower. If you plan to have a back center seam, place the T–L line on the edge of the paper, a seam allowance away from the edge (for the back seam).

To make this A-line skirt, go to "Basic A-Line Skirt" later in this chapter.

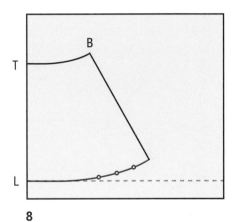

8

Wraparound Skirt Pattern

Wraparound (or wrap) skirts are similar to straight or A-line skirts except that either the front or the back is designed to overlap. Before you make the pattern, decide whether you want your skirt to be more like a straight skirt or more like an A-line skirt. If you want a straight wraparound, follow steps 1–10 of the earlier "Straight Skirt Pattern." If you want more of an A-line look, follow steps 1–8 of the earlier "A-Line Skirt Pattern."

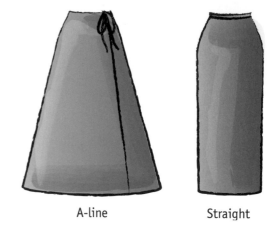

A-line   Straight

Decide if you want the skirt to overlap in the front or in the back. For example, if you want the skirt to overlap in the front, make a pattern for one back piece without a back-center seam and two full front pieces.

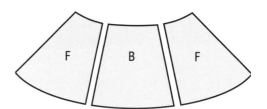

If you want the skirt to overlap in the back, make a pattern for one front piece without a front center seam and two back pieces without center back seams.

To assemble a wraparound skirt, follow the directions later in this chapter for "Basic Wrap Skirt."

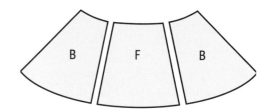

Pull-on skirts are the easiest to make: two rectangles of fabric, an encased elastic waistline, two seams and a hem, and you are good to go.

This design works well if your waistline and hip line are closer together in size. I suggest a soft, flowing fabric, such as a lightweight jersey knit or challis. Stiff and/or heavier-weight fabrics do not work as well with elastic-gathered waists.

Make the Pull-On Skirt

MATERIALS

- Pattern of rectangle. See "Design Your Own Skirt Patterns" earlier in this chapter for "Pull-On Skirt Pattern."

- 1–2 lengths of a lightweight, soft flowing fabric (A length is the length of your rectangle plus 4–6 inches.) If the fabric is wide enough for both the front and back rectangle pattern pieces to fit side by side, you may need only 1 length. It depends on how wide your rectangle is.

- ¾ to ⅞-inch wide elastic used for waists. You will need at least your waist measurement plus about 4 inches. If you use 1-inch elastic you will have to increase your waist casing by a fraction of an inch for the elastic to fit.

- Thread to match your fabric

PRE-ASSEMBLY OF PULL-ON SKIRT

Use your own pattern as suggested in the "Pull-On Skirt Pattern" section, earlier in this chapter (just one rectangle pattern piece).

1 Prepare fabric (see Chapter 2).

2 You need to cut two rectangles of the same size. If the fabric has no nap and is wide enough for the rectangle to fit, fold the fabric in half on the lengthwise grain. Place the length of the pattern rectangle on the lengthwise grain (see chapters 2 and 4) and pin in place. If the fabric is not wide enough for the rectangle pattern when the fabric is folded, then unfold it flat and cut the two rectangle pieces one at a time.

NOTE: If there is a nap, do not fold the fabric. Make sure that the tops of the rectangles are going in the same direction.

❸ Cut out each pattern piece with scissors or a rotary cutter and mat, keeping the pattern and fabric as flat and smooth as possible (see Chapter 4).

ASSEMBLY OF PULL-ON SKIRT

❶ With right sides together, sew side seams together. Finish seams (see Chapter 2). Press seams open.

❷ Stitch the seam allowance to the skirt at the top of each seam for approximately 2 inches. This will make it easier to slide the elastic through later.

❸ Make the waistline casing. Press the top edge of the skirt ¼ inch to the inside.

❹ Press the folded edge made in Step 3, 1 inch to the inside. The width of this fold should be slightly larger than the width of the elastic you are using. Pin the casing to the skirt.

❺ Topstitch the casing close to the first fold made, leaving an opening to insert the elastic just in back of one of the seams.

❻ When measuring the elastic needed, use your waist measurement plus 1 inch. Using a safety pin pinned into the end of the elastic, thread the elastic into the casing being careful not to pull the other end of the elastic into the casing. Pin the elastic ends together. Put on the skirt, and adjust the length of the elastic by repinning if necessary. Take the skirt off.

❼ Check to make sure the elastic has not twisted in the casing. Overlap and securely stitch the ends of the elastic together.

❽ Distribute the gathers evenly, keeping the side seams at your sides. Put a pin in each side seam, catching the elastic.

❾ In the side seam, attach the elastic to the casing by stitching in the ditch of the side seam (see Chapter 2). This will keep the elastic from twisting and keep the gathers evenly distributed.

❿ Hem your skirt, using one of the methods described in Chapter 5. A slit can be left in the lower edge of a side seam if the skirt length is below the knee and is needed for ease in walking.

To make a basic straight skirt, use the "Straight Skirt Pattern" suggested earlier in this chapter.

Do not worry about the waistband treatment—you can change that in a variety of ways (see Chapter 6). Also, do not worry about embellishments right now. Later in this section, you will see a variety of ways to modify a plain straight skirt.

STRAIGHT SKIRT FEATURES

Regardless of length, a straight skirt usually has the same basic features: two side seams and one back seam, if the zipper is in the back. Sometimes there are only two side seams, in which case the zipper is in the left side seam. The seams are perpendicular to the floor, and the width of the skirt at the hemline is approximately the same as the width at the hip. The hip shaping is accomplished by curving in the sides up to the smaller waistline. The tummy and rear shaping is accomplished with one or two darts, pleats, or gathers at the waist.

The darts and pleats can be eliminated altogether if your waist is as large as or larger than your hips. The darts can also be changed to gentle gathers or tiny pleats. If the skirt goes below the knee, you may want to put a slit in one or both side seams or the back seam to facilitate walking (see Chapter 5).

Follow the steps in Chapter 4, "Find the Right Fit," and adjust the pattern to fit you.

Make the Straight Skirt

MATERIALS

- Pattern pieces from earlier in this chapter for basic straight skirt

- 1 or 2 lengths of fabric. (Whether you need 1 or 2 lengths depends on the width of the fabric and the width of the pattern at its widest point.)

- 7–9 inch skirt zipper

- Thread to match fabric

- Interfacing if you are making a traditional waistband

- Button or skirt hook and eye and snap if you are making a traditional waistband

PRE-ASSEMBLY OF STRAIGHT SKIRT

The following are basic instructions for assembling a skirt.

1 Prepare and press the fabric and pattern pieces (see chapters 2 and 3).

2 Lay out the pattern pieces on the fabric. Put the pins in the seam allowance parallel to the edge of the fabric, or use pattern weights to hold the pattern pieces in place. Remember to check the grainline.

3 If you are making a traditional waistband, cut a rectangle on the lengthwise grain as long as your waist in inches plus 2-4 inches for overlap plus seam allowances and 2 times the width of the finished waistband plus seam allowances.

4 Cut out each pattern piece with scissors or a rotary cutter and mat, keeping the pattern and fabric as flat and smooth as possible. Accuracy in cutting is crucial in determining how well the various pieces of a garment will fit together (see Chapter 3).

5 If you made darts, pleats, or gathers on your pattern, transfer these markings to the cut-out fabric pieces. Darts, pleats, and dots can be marked on the wrong side of the fabric using a tracing wheel and tracing paper, a disappearing fabric marking pencil, or tailor's chalk. Choose a marking technique that is appropriate for the fabric and that will not show on the right side. (see Chapter 3).

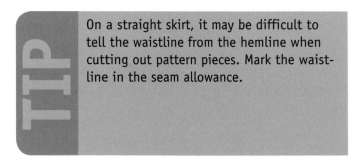

TIP

On a straight skirt, it may be difficult to tell the waistline from the hemline when cutting out pattern pieces. Mark the waistline in the seam allowance.

ASSEMBLY OF STRAIGHT SKIRT

1 Stay-stitch the waist edge within the seam allowance of each skirt piece ¼ inch in from the seam line to stabilize the waist edge and keep it from stretching during construction. If you are using a woven fabric, also stay-stitch along the edge of each seam to keep the fabric from raveling back into the seam during wear and laundering.

2 Sew the darts in place as marked or baste in pleats and gathers. If you are putting on patch pockets, put them on now.

3 For an invisible zipper, follow the directions on the package. Invisible zippers are put in before the seam is sewn. For a traditional zipper, mark where the bottom of the zipper will be in the seam. Using the regular stitch length, sew the back seam from the hem to the point marked for the bottom of the zipper. Backstitch.

Using the longest stitch length, baste the rest of the seam closed. (See Chapter 2 for more on putting in zippers, or use the directions on the package or the directions in your sewing machine manual.)

4 Sew the skirt front to the skirt back at the side seams by placing the right sides together and using the seam allowance you designed into your pattern.

5 Try on the skirt to see whether the side seams need to be let out or taken in and to make sure that the seams are under your arms and perpendicular to the floor.

6 Finish the waist edge according to one of the suggestions in Chapter 6. Finish the waist opening above the zipper with a button and buttonhole on the waistband, a snap, or a hook and eye (see Chapter 2).

7 Hem the skirt (see Chapter 5).

SLIT (OPTIONAL)

If the skirt length extends below the knees, you may want to allow for a slit in the seam at the hem edge. You can choose either one slit in the back seam or a slit in one or both of the side seams. Leave the seam open from the hem edge to whatever length you want. Using a ¼-inch double-fold hem, either hand-slip-stitch or machine-stitch the seam allowances to the inside, beginning at the top of the opening.

Variations on the Straight Skirt

RUFFLE

From the same fabric or a contrasting fabric, add a ruffle or two to the bottom of the skirt (see Chapter 5 on ruffles). The ruffle will add length to the skirt, so shorten your skirt by the same amount as the finished width of the ruffle being added. If your fabric is stiff or heavyweight, a slight ruffle works best if you are making it from the same fabric. In general, softer fabrics with more drape work well as ruffles. If you add more than one ruffle, the ruffles do not even need to be from the same fabric!

FLOUNCE

From the same fabric or a contrasting fabric, add a flounce or two (see Chapter 5). The flounce will add length to the skirt, so shorten your skirt by the same amount as the finished width of the flounce being added. Flounces can be any width just like ruffles. However, flounces do not have a gathered top edge as ruffles do. A flounce gives a skirt a slightly more formal look than a ruffle.

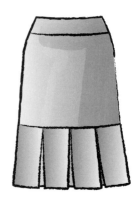

BAND

Using a contrasting fabric and/or color, attach a band of any width as if it were a "waistband" but attached to the *hem* of the skirt (see Chapter 6). If the band is very wide, (more than 6 inches), make it a single layer, attaching one edge to the skirt and hemming the other edge. When attaching the band, match any band seams to the skirt side and back seams. Adding this band will lengthen your skirt, so plan accordingly by shortening the skirt equal to the width of the finished band.

If it is a long skirt with a back seam slit, you may want to add a slit to the bottom band at the back seam also. See "Slit (Optional)" on the previous page.

Basic A-Line Skirt

Over the last half-century, the basic A-line skirt introduced by Christian Dior has undergone some variations. The dress/skirt first introduced had all the shaping in the two side seams and one back seam, which created a funnel shape. Women's waistlines were much narrower then, causing sweeping full skirts. They also had flatter tummies because they wore girdles. Gabrielle Chanel simplified the style by pulling in the diagonal lines of the funnel shape so that the skirt was not as full.

Make the A-Line Skirt

A-LINE SKIRT FEATURES

Today, *A-line* refers to a skirt that is narrower at the hip than at the hemline. Of course, an A-line can vary from almost straight to almost flared. Keep in mind that the general look is to be an A with the side seams going diagonally from the waist to the hem. Most of the shaping is in the seam lines, keeping tummy and rear darts, pleats, and gathers to a minimum.

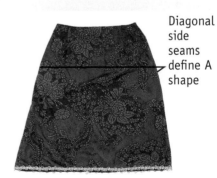

Diagonal side seams define A shape

MATERIALS

- Pattern pieces you designed earlier in the "A-Line Skirt Pattern" section

- 1 or 2 lengths of fabric. If there is no nap, one of the pattern pieces can be placed right side up and the other upside down. If the skirt is not too wide at the hem, you may need only 1 length. If the fabric has nap, you will need 2 lengths so they can both be placed with the top in the same direction.

- 7-9 inch skirt zipper

- Interfacing if you are making a traditional waistband

- Button, or skirt hook and eye and snap for waist band

- Thread to match fabric

PRE-ASSEMBLY OF A-LINE SKIRT

The following are basic instructions for assembling an A-line skirt.

1. Prepare and press the fabric and pattern pieces (see Chapters 2 and 3).

2. Lay out the pattern pieces on the fabric. Put the pins in the seam allowance parallel to the edge of the fabric, or use pattern weights to hold the pattern pieces in place. Don't forget to check the grainline. If you are making a traditional waistband, cut a rectangle on the lengthwise grain as long as your waist in inches plus 2-4 inches for overlap plus seam allowances and 2 times the width of the finished waistband plus seam allowances.

3. Cut out each pattern piece with scissors or a rotary cutter and mat, keeping the pattern and fabric as flat and smooth as possible. Accuracy in cutting is crucial in determining how well the various pieces of a garment will fit together (see Chapter 3).

4. If you made darts, pleats, or gathers on your pattern, transfer these markings to the cut-out fabric pieces. Darts, pleats, and dots can be marked on the wrong side of the fabric using a tracing wheel and tracing paper, a disappearing fabric marking pencil, or tailor's chalk. Choose a marking technique that is appropriate for the fabric and that will not show on the right side (see Chapter 3).

ASSEMBLY OF A-LINE SKIRT

1. Stay-stitch the waist edge within the seam allowance of each skirt piece ¼ inch in from the seam line to stabilize the waist edge and keep it from stretching during construction. If you are using a woven fabric, also stay-stitch along the edge of each seam to keep it from raveling back into the seam during wear and laundering.

2. If you had to include darts, pleats or gathers when you made your mock-up, sew them in now. If you are putting on patch pockets, put them on now.

③ For an invisible zipper, follow the directions on the package. Invisible zippers are put in before the seam is sewn. For a traditional zipper, mark where the bottom of the zipper will be in the seam. Using the regular stitch length, sew the back seam from the hem to the point marked for the bottom of the zipper. Backstitch.

Using the longest stitch length, baste the rest of the seam closed. (See Chapter 2 for more on putting in zippers, or use the directions on the package or the directions in your sewing machine manual.)

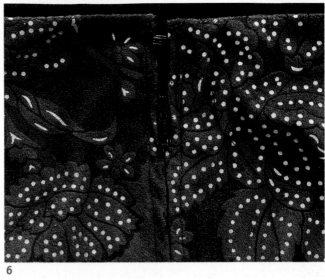

6

④ Sew the skirt front to the skirt back at the side seams by placing the right sides together and using the seam allowance you designed into your pattern.

⑤ Try on the skirt to see whether the side seams need to be let out or taken in.

⑥ Finish the waist edge according to one of the suggestions in Chapter 6. Finish the waist opening above the zipper with a button and buttonhole, a snap, or a hook and eye (see Chapter 2).

⑦ Hem the skirt (see Chapter 5).

The variations for the A-line skirt are similar to those for the basic straight skirt (see section "Variations on the Straight Skirt" earlier in this chapter).

Basic Wraparound Skirt

If you want to make one of the easiest skirts to get into and out of, try a wraparound. It requires more fabric because you have to make either two fronts or two backs. While more popular in the late twentieth century than in the early twenty-first century, wrap skirts are still very versatile and are great for both casual and formal occasions. They are particularly useful as beach attire—easy on, easy off.

WRAP SKIRT FEATURES

A basic wrap skirt does not have a zipper. The wrapped section is usually in the front, occasionally in the back, and the skirt's open sections are closed by ties, buttons, snaps, or hooks and eyes. A typical wrap skirt has one back piece and two front pieces, one of which overlaps the other. The front (or back) overlapped sections are not sewn together and need to be finished similar to a hem. If you are using ties, you also need a slit (buttonhole) in the waistband for one of the ties to go through.

Waistband   Buttonhole   Tie

Wrap skirt patterns may vary from straight to A-lines. Wrap skirts are much more forgiving in terms of fit, particularly if you use ties to hold the skirt together. When adjusting the pattern to fit you, remember that the side seams should be under your arms (see Chapter 4, "Find the Right Fit").

The amount of wrap is up to your taste and design inclinations. If you choose ties to close the skirt, it will be easier if you have a waistband (see Chapter 6).

Make the Wrap Skirt

MATERIALS

- The "Wrap Skirt Pattern" described earlier in this chapter

- 2 lengths of fabric

- Interfacing if you want a traditional waistband with ties

- Buttons, snaps, or hooks and eyes, if you do not want a tie waistband

- Snaps or hook and loop tape for inside fastening

- Thread to match your fabric

PRE-ASSEMBLY OF WRAP SKIRT

The following are basic instructions for assembling a wrap skirt.

1 Prepare and press the fabric and pattern pieces (see chapters 2 and 3).

2 Lay out the pattern pieces on the fold of the fabric according to figure at right. Put the pins in the seam allowance parallel to the edge of the fabric, or use pattern weights to hold the pattern pieces in place. Don't forget to check the grainline. If you are making a traditional waistband, cut a rectangle on the lengthwise grain as long as your waist in inches plus 2–4 inches for overlap plus seam allowances and 2 times the width of the finished waistband plus seam allowances. If you want ties, cut two more rectangles long enough for ties. See Chapter 5 on ties for more detailed information.

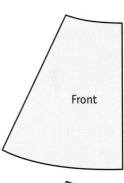

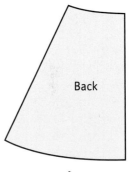

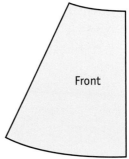

③ Cut out each pattern piece with scissors or a rotary cutter and mat, keeping the pattern and fabric as flat and smooth as possible (see Chapter 3).

④ If you made darts, pleats, or gathers on your pattern, transfer these markings to the cut-out fabric pieces. Darts, pleats, and dots can be marked on the wrong side of the fabric using a tracing wheel and tracing paper, a disappearing fabric marking pencil, or tailor's chalk. Choose a marking technique that is appropriate for the fabric and that will not show on the right side (see Chapter 3).

ASSEMBLY OF WRAP SKIRT

Follow the directions below for putting a basic wrap skirt together. For variations on the wrap skirt, follow the suggestions for the straight skirt or A-line skirt above.

① Follow steps 1, 2, and 4 for straight skirt assembly.

⑤ Finish the open edges of the front pieces. Use one of the methods suggested in Chapter 5.

⑥ With right sides together, sew the skirt front pieces to the skirt back at the side seams.

⑦ If you are making a tie waistband, follow the directions for a tie waistband in Chapter 6. Put a buttonhole in the waistband just in back of the right side seam so that the tie can go through, wrap around the back to the left side, where it can be tied to the tie on the front extension.

⑧ If you are using buttons and buttonholes, finish the waist edge from one of the options in Chapter 6.
Put in buttonholes on the right hand edge on the piece that overlaps and buttons on the underlap. Sew a snap or hook-and-loop tape at the open-edge waist of the underlap and on the overlap where it meets the open edge of the underlap (right inside).

⑨ Hem the wrap skirt using one of the methods in Chapter 5.

Basic Tiered Skirt

ere is another opportunity to be creative or go a little wild. This skirt is easy to make but takes longer to put together than some other skirts because of all the ruffles (tiers) involved. These skirts tend to flow, so softer fabrics are preferable to stiffer ones. Depending on your personality and body shape, you can calculate the size and fullness of each layer (tier), or you can just guess within some minor parameters and let it happen.

TIERED SKIRT FEATURES

Think rectangles! The top rectangle goes around your waist. If this rectangle is narrow, any amount of fabric wider than your waist measurement will work. If the top rectangle is long enough to reach your hips, then the rectangle has to be any amount wider than your hip measurement.

As you descend down the skirt, each rectangle will be fuller (have more fabric in it) than the previous rectangle to which it will be attached. The tiers also can change in length (see the "Materials" section that follows). You can choose to have as many tiers as you want, made from whatever fabrics you want (they do not even need to match), and arrange the lengths in any way you want. How long you make this skirt is a matter of choice. There are no rules!

Tier 1

Tier 2

Tier 3

Make the Tiered Skirt

Before you start, you should decide the order and the number of tiers, as well as the length of each tier.

MATERIALS

- Several soft fabrics that appeal to you.

NOTE: These skirts are deceiving. They require more fabric than you might guess at first. Even though you do not need a pattern to make this skirt, you may want to check a pattern book for amounts of fabric to purchase.

> For the skirt pictured on the previous page, the first (top) tier is 1½ widths of fabric. If you have a narrower hip than 44 inches, you may only need 1 width of fabric. The second tier is 2 widths of fabric. The third tier is 2½ widths of fabric, and the fourth tier is 3 widths of fabric. The optional bottom ruffle is 4 widths of fabric.

- 1-inch waist elastic long enough to go around your waist, plus a few inches for overlap. (The elastic will be in a casing at the waist, so you do not have to be precise as to your waist measurement).

- Thread to match your fabric.

PRE-ASSEMBLY OF TIERED SKIRT

1. Prepare the fabric (see Chapter 2).

2. Cut out all the rectangles you need (see "Tiered Skirt Features," earlier in this section, for suggestions). This is when a rotary cutter and a mat come in very handy.

> **TIP**
>
> All the seams of tiers, except the top tier, can be positioned anywhere. Try to position them in different places rather than on top of each other. Decide how you want to finish the top and bottom of each ruffle (tier). For options, see the "Ruffles" section in Chapter 5.

ASSEMBLY OF TIERED SKIRT

① Sew the vertical end seams of each individual tier together, making several big circles, and then press the seams open.

② Sew a gathering stitch around the top of all the tiers except the top one by lengthening the stitch length on your sewing machine and not backstitching when you begin or end the stitching. See Chapter 5 for more information on gathering.

③ Sew the top of the second tier circle to the bottom of the first tier circle. First, you will have to pull up the gathering thread to gather the second tier circle, distributing the gathers evenly so that it fits the bottom edge of the top-tier circle. Use a lot of pins to pin the two tiers together.

Continue in this manner, sewing the top of the third-tier circle to the bottom of the second-tier circle, until all your tier circles have been sewn together.

④ Make a casing at the waist edge of the skirt using one of the methods suggested in Chapter 6. Note you may sew the casing in the top tier before Step 5, but put the elastic in after you finish sewing all the tiers together.

⑤ Finish the hem edge of the bottom tier using one of the methods suggested in Chapter 5. You may want to finish the hem edge before you attach the last tier to the skirt. It will be easier to handle.

CHAPTER 9

Pants

Pants are a relatively new fashion item for women, historically speaking, but since their introduction they have varied greatly in length, style, and name. There are a host of pants patterns on the market. If you are new to sewing, find a pants pattern that is *easy to sew*. Don't try to make highly tailored trousers or jeans with front fly zipper openings as your first pants project. An example of an easy basic pants pattern that can be made quickly would be a pair of elastic waist pull-on pants that only has two pattern pieces: front and back.

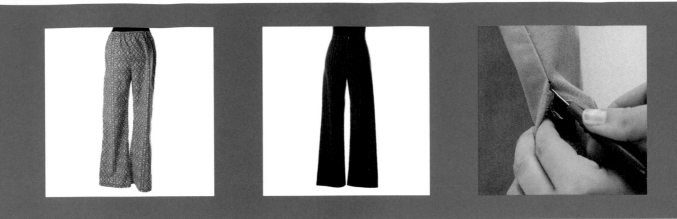

Pant Lengths, Shapes, and Styles

Just as skirts come in various lengths, styles, fabrics, and fullnesses, so do pants, from short shorts to palazzos. Even with all the variations, you still have to decide how you want to finish the waistline and hemline, how long or short or narrow or full you want your pants to be, and what fabric to choose.

LENGTHS

Some pant names give an indication of the length of the pant leg, such as *shorts*. However, there are variations of length even within the shorts category.

Some shorts are short shorts with just enough leg to call them pants, while *Bermuda shorts* have the hem of the legs just above the knee. Bermuda shorts are much more formal in design than most other shorts and can be worn instead of pants to more upscale events. During World War II, the British government did not have enough fabric to make long pants for their soldiers, so they redesigned the uniforms to have shorter pant legs. The style caught on for general wear in Bermuda (a British colony), hence its commonly known name.

Pedal pushers, which were very popular during the 1940s, came into fashion for riding bikes. The length of the leg stopped at about mid-calf. This prevented the pants from getting caught in a bicycle's gear chain. Pedal pushers had enough ease to make it easy to move one's knees in order to pedal. For the most part, pedal pushers have been replaced by *capris*. The length of the leg is about the same, mid-calf, but in general capris have less ease and fit tighter, particularly around the calf. An East Coast variation of pedal pushers/capris are called *clam diggers*. They have a turned-up cuff to simulate turning up your pant legs in order to wade into the water and dig for clams.

The terms *pants* and *trousers* usually relate to pants that just brush the shoe. Trousers tend to be more upscale and formal, while pants tend to be more everyday.

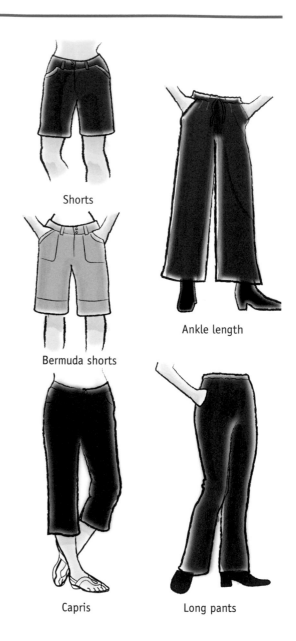

Shorts

Bermuda shorts

Ankle length

Capris

Long pants

STYLES

In addition to being identified by length, pants are also referred to by various styles of the legs, seat, and waist. For example, *bell bottoms* are pants with straight or narrow legs that "bell" out at the bottom hem—the hemline being wider than any other part of the leg.

Culottes come in a variety of lengths, but look like a skirt at first glance because the legs are so wide. *Skorts*, a variation on culottes, are shorts with a front panel that make it look like a skirt from the front and shorts from the back.

Overalls are pants that have a great deal of ease, can be worn over other garments, and usually have a "bib" and straps.

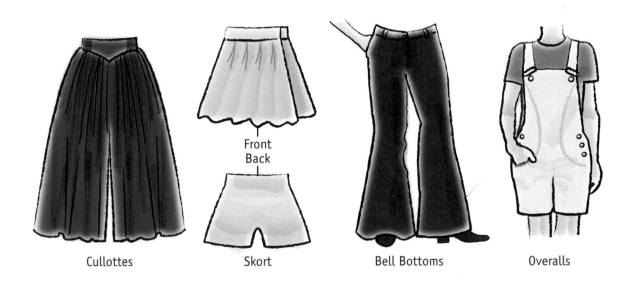

Cullottes

Front
Back

Skort

Bell Bottoms

Overalls

FABRICS

Pants are also known by the fabric. *Chinos* are made from a twill fabric, usually made from cotton. They are lightweight and comfortable to wear. *Jeans* or *dungarees* are made from denim—a very sturdy fabric that takes a great deal of wear and tear; the more they are washed, the better they look. *Cords* are made from corduroy, and *sweats* are made from stretchy "sweatshirt" cotton fabric.

Sweats   Jeans   Chinos   Cords

M any types of casual pants can be made quickly and easily with an elastic waist. The elastic waist eliminates the need for darts and a zipper. Elastic-waist pants also have enough ease that the exact fit is not as important. The idea is comfort. Examples of comfortable elastic-waist pull-on pants would include sweatpants or pajama pants. The photo shows a pair of elastic-waist pull-on pants with a fold-down waist casing.

Construct Elastic-Waist Pull-On Pants

MATERIALS

When choosing the fabric for casual elastic-waist pant, consider using a knit. That will eliminate the need to stay-stitch the seams since knits don't ravel. Also take into consideration that if you use a woven fabric, there will be some gathers at the waistline, so you may not want to choose a very stiff fabric.

- If the fabric is wide so that the front and back pattern pieces can be placed side by side, 1 length of fabric equal to the overall length of the pattern piece should be enough—approximately $1\frac{3}{8}$–$2\frac{1}{4}$ yards.

- You will need 2 lengths if the fabric has a nap or is too narrow for the front and back pattern pieces to go side by side. A length of fabric for pants is the number of inches from your waist to where you want the bottom of the pants to be, plus hem and waistline casing—approximately $2\frac{1}{8}$–$2\frac{5}{8}$ yards.

- Thread to match or contrast with the fabric

- Enough waistband elastic to go around your waist plus 2 inches. Soft sport elastic works well for these casual pants. The elastic should be just a bit narrower than the width of the casing.

- Large paper marked in 1-inch squares on which to draw the pattern.

TIP

Fabric stores are always having sales on notions. Various kinds and widths of elastic are good to keep on hand in your supply drawer.

CREATE A PATTERN

Follow the front and back diagrams for an approximation of a generic pair of pull-on pants. Notice the extra length at the top of the waist for a turned-down casing for elastic. The waist measurement should be 2–4 inches larger than your hips. Transfer the diagram to the large paper. Adjust the waist and hip for your size. Don't forget to add 2–4 inches of ease overall. See Chapter 4 for alterations to make your pants pattern fit.

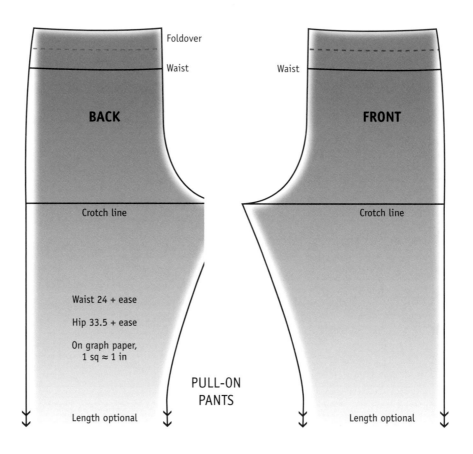

Foldover

Waist   Waist

BACK   **FRONT**

Crotch line   Crotch line

Waist 24 + ease

Hip 33.5 + ease

On graph paper,
1 sq ≈ 1 in

PULL-ON
PANTS

Length optional   Length optional

PRE-ASSEMBLY OF ELASTIC-WAIST PULL-ON PANTS

Listed below are the general steps involved in putting together a pair of elastic-waist pull-on pants with a fold-down waist casing:

1 Prepare the fabric (see Chapter 1).

2 Follow the general directions for laying out a pattern and cutting pieces in chapters 3 and 4. Make a mock-up from muslin or scrap fabrics as described in Chapter 4. Be sure to mark the pieces, top, bottom, right, left, inside, and outside.

3 Try on the muslin. Does the waistline of the pants fit over your hips? Is there enough ease around the hips—or is there too much? Is the crotch line where you want it to be? See chapter 4 for more specific suggestions for getting a comfortable fit.

4 When you are satisfied with the fit, pull the basting threads, take the muslin pieces apart, and use the muslin pieces as the pattern for your garment or transfer the changes to your paper pattern. Check to be sure the grainlines are straight. Cut out the pieces.

ASSEMBLY OF ELASTIC-WAIST PULL-ON PANTS

1 If you want to add a patch pocket to the front or back of the pants, make it as described in Chapter 12 and topstitch it in place.

2 With right sides together, stitch the pants front leg to the pants back leg along the inner leg seams $5/8$-inch seam.

3 Press each seam to set the stitches, and then press the seams open.

4 With right sides together, sew the center front and back crotch seam together, matching inner leg seams. Stitch a second row of stitching about $1/4$-inch inside the seam allowance to reinforce the lower crotch seam several inches on both sides of the inseam.

5 Trim out this area of the crotch seam close to the second row of stitching and press the rest of the center front and center back seams open above the reinforced stitching.

6 With right sides together, sew the front to the back at the side seams. Press to set the stitches and press the seam open.

7 Try on the pants to double-check the fit before finishing. Tie a ¼-inch-wide piece of elastic around your waist to hold the pants in place with the extra length for the casing at the top of the pants folded down over the elastic to see if the crotch depth is too short or too long and that there is room to sit down comfortably in your pants. See Chapter 4 for more detail on fitting your pants.

8 Make a casing wide enough for your elastic. Feed the elastic through the casing. (See Chapter 6 for more on casings.)

9 Hem the pants. (See Chapter 5 for more on hems.)

VARIATION: DRAWSTRING PANTS

If you'd like to use a drawstring instead of elastic in the casing, see chapters 6 and 7. You will need to make a buttonhole or put in two grommets to put the drawstring through. For the buttonhole, see chapters 2 and 6. For grommets, you will need a special tool, which usually comes with directions and the grommets.

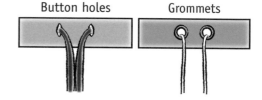

Button holes   Grommets

If you make a tie greater than 2–4 inches wide, use a buttonhole; for cording, use grommets.

Before turning down the waistline casing, press the front waistband in half from side to side. Mark the center point. On each side of the center point, put a mark about 1 inch on each side and centered from top fold to waist seam line on the half of the waistline casing that will be visible to the public.

Fitted pants can be any length. They may have darts or pleats, a waistband, and a zipper or button closure. They may also have patch, inseam, or slant pockets. A fairly firm woven fabric is a good choice for a basic fitted pant. Unlike pull-ons, basic fitted pants fit snugly around the waist, hips, seat, and crotch. The pants included here have a facing for the fitted waist instead of the waistband. Feel free to replace the facing with any width waistband. The centered zipper is in the back seam.

Construct a Pair of Fitted Pants

MATERIALS

- 1 or 2 lengths of fabric, depending on the width of the fabric, your size, the length of the pants, and whether the fabric has a nap. (See the previous pull-on pants materials list for definition of fabric length.)

- Thread to match your fabric
- 7–9-inch traditional zipper to match your fabric

CREATE A PATTERN

Using the generic pattern shown on the following page (right), draw a pattern on large paper. Adjust the hip line to fit you, plus 2–3 inches of design ease. The waist measurement will be adjusted by darts, pleats, or gathers. The length of the pants is up to you. Follow the instructions in Chapter 4 for adjusting the crotch curve.

Also make a waistline facing. It may be easier to do so after you have made the pants and have adjusted them for size. Make a single front facing and two back facings (if you have chosen to put the zipper in the back). Follow the curve of the pants' waistline. Don't forget to include seam allowances. See Chapter 6 on making your own facing.

PRE-ASSEMBLY OF FITTED PANTS

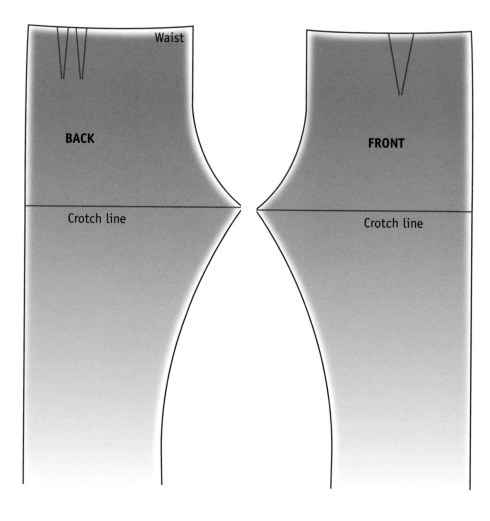

1 Prepare and press the fabric and pattern as described in chapters 1 and 3.

2 Make a mock-up of the pattern from fabric scraps or muslin and adjust pattern to fit your body. (See chapters 3 and 4.)

3 Remove the basting stitches to take apart your muslin. Use your muslin as a pattern (or transfer the changes to your paper pattern), making sure to keep the grainline straight, and cut out the pieces from your fabric. Mark all the pieces very carefully. Be precise with your markings. Also mark the public (right) side and the wrong side of each piece of fabric and the tops and bottoms. It is so easy to end up with a funny-looking pair of pants with a crotch seam sticking out. Fronts and backs, rights and lefts, insides and outsides all begin to look alike!

4 Stay-stitch the seam edges of woven fabric to keep them from raveling.

Put Together a Pair of Basic Fitted Pants

1 Sew the darts and/or pleats in place (see Chapter 2) and press.

If your pants have patch pockets, you would put them on next. Most fitted pants do not have patch pockets.

2 On both legs, stitch front to back at the inner leg seam.

3 With right sides together, stitch the pants center front seam together continuing from the bottom of the zipper opening in the back center seam to the front center seam. This is the crotch seam. Stitch a second row of stitching about ¼ inch inside the seam allowance to reinforce the lower crotch seam several inches on both sides of the inseam. Trim out the area of the lower crotch seam close to the second row of stitching and press the rest of the center front and center back seams open above the reinforced stitching.

4 Put in the zipper (see Chapter 4).

5 With right sides together, sew the front to the back at the side seams. Press to set the stitches and then press the seams open.

6 Interface the facing. Finish the lower raw edge of the facing. With right sides together, stitch the facing to the waist. Clip, press, and under-stitch. Neatly tuck in the ends of the facing under the wrong side at the zipper and slip-stitch in place.

NOTE: Stitch the facing to the pants by stitching in the ditch in the side seams. See Chapter 6 for more on waistline facings.

7 Finish the pant bottom hems according to the pattern directions or the suggestions in Chapter 5.

Variations for a Pair of Basic Fitted Pants

Once you have made a basic pair of pants that fits well and is comfortable to wear, you can reuse that basic pattern for basically all of your pants, with some of the following variations.

CHANGE THE LEGS

You can vary the pattern by changing the length to shorts, Bermudas, or capris. Vary the style by changing the width of the leg from tapered to straight or flared.

Straight-leg pants are the same width at the hem as at the knee, with the side and inseams going straight down to the hem. To make the leg a little narrower at the hem than at the knee (make sure the hem isn't too small to fit comfortably over your foot), gradually taper in both sides and inseams the same amount to keep the grainline straight by placing a yardstick diagonally from the knee to the smaller hem and mark a new cutting line.

To flare the leg, mark a new cutting line, tracing the yardstick angled out wider at the hemline than the knee at both the inseam and the side seams to keep the grainline straight.

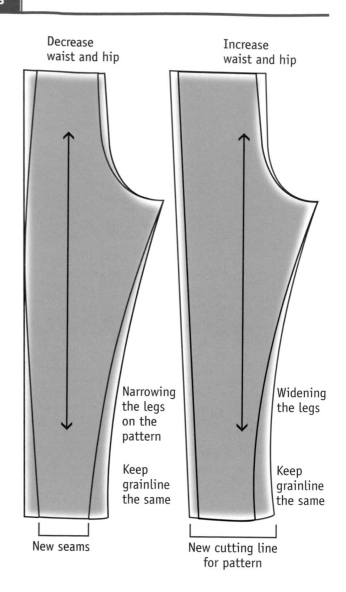

Decrease waist and hip

Increase waist and hip

Narrowing the legs on the pattern

Keep grainline the same

New seams

Widening the legs

Keep grainline the same

New cutting line for pattern

If the legs are tapered so that they are narrower at the hem than a straight-leg pant leg would be, taper the leg hem allowance at the bottom edge of the legs back out slightly wider for about an inch (or the depth of the hem allowance if it is more than an inch). This will give you enough fabric to fold the hem allowance up without causing puckers.

GATHER THE BACK OF THE WAISTBAND

This waistband is often used with a fitted pair of pants that has a center front zipper opening. It is also useful for a pull-on pair of pants that doesn't have much fullness at the waist so that a traditional waistband can be used in the front and an elastic waistband in the back for a less casual look and breathable comfort.

Leave the back darts unsewn. Make a waistband the length of the new back waistline. Sew the back waistband to the front waistband at the side seams. Sew the waistband to pants in the traditional manner, matching side seams (see Chapter 6).

Once the waistband has been attached, open the side seams on the inside only. Insert elastic to fit your back waist. Sew the ends of the elastic into the side seams using the stitch in the ditch (see Chapter 2). Restitch the opening in the side seams with hand stitches as described in Chapter 2.

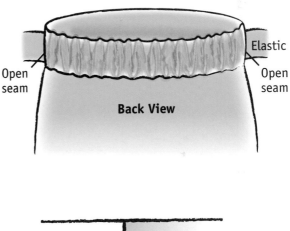

Back View

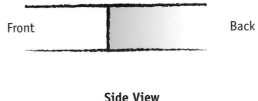

Side View

ADD SLITS

Follow the directions for slits in Chapter 8 under straight skirts. Slits can go in the side seams of any length of pants, but are most often found in mid-calf-length capris to allow the knee to bend.

INSERT ELASTIC OR TIES IN LEG HEMS

You can turn just-below-the-knee-length pants into knickerbockers or full-length pants into pantaloons by inserting elastic in a casing at the bottom of the straight leg. Or add ties to the bottoms of any length leg by putting a slit in the side seam and by inserting a tie in the "hem" casing.

Knickerbockers

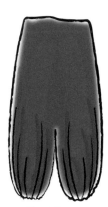

Pantaloons

GODETS

A *godet* is a triangular piece of fabric, sometimes with a rounded bottom, that is inserted into a seam. Godets can be inserted into skirt seams or bottom side seams of pants. See Chapter 12 for specific instructions for adding godets.

TRIM OR EMBELLISH

Go wild, have fun—the number and kinds of trims available today are almost infinite. You can use any type of trim, from lace to rhinestones, to add pizzazz to a pair of pants. The sky and your imagination are the only limits to how pants can be embellished. See Chapter 12 for more ideas.

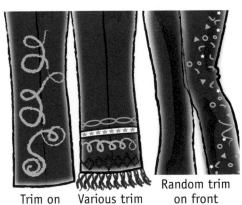

Trim on side seam Various trim on leg bottom Random trim on front of one leg

Design a Pair of Pants by Deconstruction

The trickiest part of designing a pair of pants from scratch without a commercial pattern is drawing the depth, length, and curvature of the crotch line. Getting this line exactly right for your body shape takes a little trial and error. One of the easiest ways to come close the first time is to use an existing pair of pants that fits you well.

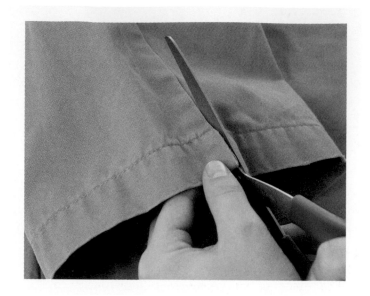

Materials

- 1 pair of pants that fits you well, without front or back yokes
- Approximately 2 lengths of fabric (use your pants to estimate the amount of fabric you will need)
- Thread to match
- Large paper with 1-inch squares
- A 7–9-inch matching zipper (optional)

Make the Pattern

You have two alternatives: You can carefully take apart a pair of comfortable, well-fitting pants you no longer wear, using the pieces for your pattern (as shown in the above photo), or you can trace the pieces onto paper without taking the pants apart first (as described below).

FOLDED OPTION

① Fold your favorite pants with the outside seam and the inseam lying straight and smooth and the front crotch pointing out to the front. Trace on a large piece of paper down the center front, around the crotch curve and down the inseam. Readjust the back leg fullness so that the side seam is lying flat (as the back leg is usually a little wider than the front leg) and trace the side seam and waistline for the front piece.

② Refold the pants with the crotch pointing to the back; draw the back pattern piece. Don't forget to add seam allowance, hem allowance, and waist treatment allowance to each piece.

DECONSTRUCTED OPTIONS

Before you take apart your pants, label each piece clearly, top, bottom, right (public) side, wrong side, and left and right leg.

OPTION 1

① Cut all the pieces apart on the seam lines: waist, zipper (if there is one), center front and back, inseam, outer leg seam, and waistband (if there is one).

② Cut darts and remove pockets.

③ Press the pieces flat.

④ Trace each piece on large paper. Label each pattern piece. Add seam allowance to all edges.

OPTION 2

1 Undo all seams carefully with a seam ripper, including darts.

2 The seam allowances will be obvious, but note the size of the seam allowances on different pieces. Mark the darts.

3 Press the pieces flat.

4 Trace each piece on large paper. Label each pattern piece. Mark the seam allowances as they are on the original.

MAKE A MUSLIN MOCK-UP

Using the pattern pieces you made, make a pair of pants from muslin (see Chapter 4 on making a muslin). Reinforce the crotch, following Step 4 for the pull-on pants earlier in this chapter.

Because you are making a pattern from a pair of pants that fits you, you will not have to make many alterations to the muslin. Here are a few reminders to check before cutting the pants fabric:

- The crotch line is the most important line on a pants pattern. The front and back crotch lines do not have the same amount of curvature. How pants fit on you depends on the size and shape of your rear and tummy. It is important to prepare the crotch seam in your muslin mock-up in order to get a comfortable fit. See Chapter 4 for adjusting the depth of the crotch and reshaping or lowering the crotch curve if necessary.

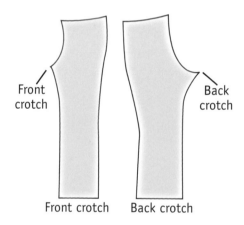

Front crotch

Back crotch

Front crotch   Back crotch

- Make adjustments to fit the pants to your body type. To make the waist smaller, add tummy and rear darts, gathers, or pleats. See Chapter 4 for more information on pants fitting.

- For a larger waistline, increase the front, back, and side seams by an equal amount, keeping the crotch curve the same.

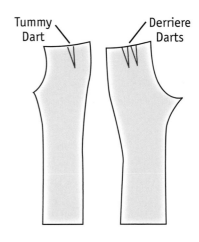

- You can adjust the leg and hip size by reshaping the side seams and/or the inside leg seams. See Chapter 4 and "Variations for a Pair of Fitted Pants" previously in this chapter for more on adjusting the leg and thigh area to keep the grainline straight down the leg.

- You can increase or decrease the hip size by increasing or decreasing the side seam in the hip area and gradually blending the new line back into the side seam above and below the hip area.

NOTE: As you change the other lines, remember to keep the crotch shape the same once you have it fit to your body type.

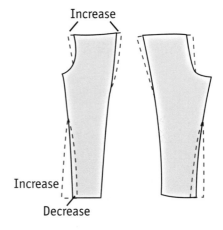

TIP

Pants made from the same basic pattern can look quite different if you vary the fabric and the amount of design ease. For other modifications, see the variations under the pattern for fitted pants.

CHAPTER 10

Tops

There are almost as many different types of tops as there are grains of sand on a beach, and there are almost as many names for the different parts of tops, from the neckline to the sleeves. The names and styles also vary by culture, geography, and climate. However, in spite of all the seasonal and regional variations, almost every top shares some basic fashion concepts: the neckline, hemline, sleeves, closure, and, most important for women, shaping for the bust. In this chapter are some sewing and design techniques to help you create tops that you love and that look terrific on you. You can mix and match, explore, experiment, and leap out of the box. By learning just a few basic concepts and techniques, you'll be able to sew a wardrobe of stylish tops. If you are starting without a commercial pattern, try one of the tops described in this chapter. There are no darts to worry about. The bust is accommodated with extra fabric to create ease.

The variation on tops is almost limitless. Below are a few of the more popular designs. At the end of this chapter, you will find directions for three of the easiest and quickest tops to put together.

- **Blouse:** A top, with or without sleeves, that is constructed from a soft, flowing fabric. Often buttons down the front; sometimes the back. The hemline often tucks into the waistline.

- **Shirt:** Usually has a collar, buttons down the front, sleeves with cuffs, and often one breast pocket. The lines are not flowing, but straighter. There may be a yoke across the back shoulders. Western shirts also have a yoke across the chest. Longer than a blouse, the hem may reach the hip line with slits or a curved bottom edge to accommodate the hips. Worn tucked in or out.

- **Tank top:** Often constructed from knit fabric with a deep scoop neck in the front and the back and no sleeves. There are usually no darts or other shaping features. The bottom is a simple hem.

- **Shell:** Constructed of soft fabric, often only two pieces, a front and a back. The neckline is usually round or boatneck. The bottom is finished with a simple hem.

- **Summer top:** Rarely has sleeves, usually one or two spaghetti straps. Sometimes strapless. No collar. Designed in various shapes, from fancy bikini bras to triangular "neckerchiefs" to elasticized shirring.

- **Tunic:** A long shirt or blouse that extends below the hip line. May pass as a shirt dress.

- **Big shirt:** Similar to a shirt, except extra large and roomy. The bottom of the shirt is not tucked in. When constructed of heavier fabric, can often substitute for a jacket.

Other tops include jackets, vests, boleros, and shrugs.

Blouse

Shirt

Tank top

Shell

Summer top

Tunic

Big shirt

Because the human body is curvy and three-dimensional and fabric is two-dimensional, fashion designers developed methods for shaping garments, particularly women's tops. The amount of design ease coupled with the drape of fabrics and a few sewing techniques determine how the bust shaping, in particular, is accommodated. Some of these sewing techniques include darts, gathers, tucks, pleats, and yokes.

DARTS

There are three typical locations for darts in tops and dresses. The wide end of the dart can begin in the shoulder seam, the underarm seam, or the waist. Regardless of where the dart starts, the point of the dart points to and ends 1 inch from the pointiest part of the breast. (See Chapter 2 for general information about darts.)

If you are using a commercial pattern, you may have to adjust the bust darts to fit your shape. Patterns are designed for a B cup size unless otherwise indicated. (See Chapter 4 for information on how to increase or decrease the cup size.) A wider dart will be necessary to give more fullness for a larger bust. You also do not want an underarm dart, for example, to point to your chin or your navel.

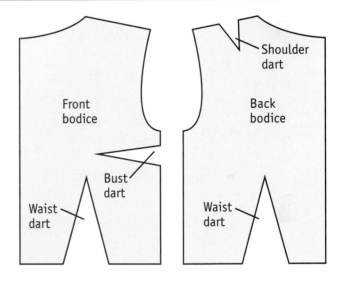

Front bodice

Bust dart

Waist dart

Shoulder dart

Back bodice

Waist dart

GATHERS, TUCKS, AND PLEATS

Gathers, tucks, and pleats can be substituted for darts beginning in the shoulder seam. You will probably want to eliminate any other darts.

Gathers give a top a softer look than darts, while tucks and pleats add a slightly more formal or sophisticated look.

YOKES

A yoke is a separate piece that is often found at the top of a skirt, pants, dress, or top. The yoke lies flat against the body and has few, if any, shaping darts. The shaping is designed into the seam that attaches the rest of the garment to the yoke, or the garment may have soft gathers or pleats where it attaches to the yoke.

Make a Boatneck Top

You can whip up this quickie boatneck top in less than two hours. You can make several tops, varying the fabric and/or length. Start with one or two rectangles and in a few minutes, you'll have a very comfortable simple top. It works best with a soft woven fabric or a knit fabric so that the front neckline drapes nicely. A stiff or heavy fabric won't drape very well.

Fabric with No Nap

MATERIALS

- 2 lengths of a soft fabric. (A length of fabric is from your shoulders to somewhere between your hips and waist, depending on how long you want the top to be.)

NOTE: If the fabric is 60 inches wide and you are small, you might need only one length.

- Matching thread
- A yardstick
- Your waist (W) and bust (B) measurements
- The length (L) you want the top to be

CUT THE FABRIC

❶ Cut a rectangle of fabric 3 or 4 inches (depending on how much ease you want) wider than half your hip or bust measurement, whichever is larger, and 2 times the length from your neck to where you want the bottom edge of the top to be.

❷ Fold the fabric in half widthwise and then lengthwise. Mark the center point on the fold.

❸ Unfold the lengthwise fold (see diagram on following page). Starting at the point marked in Step 2, cut on the widthwise fold about 4 inches in either direction. Try it on. If it goes over your head, you don't have to cut any more. If it doesn't, continue cutting equally in both directions, increasing the opening by ½-inch increments. Stop when you can easily fit your head through the hole.

ASSEMBLE THE NO-NAP BOATNECK TOP

1. With right sides together and measuring from the top (shoulder) fold, begin sewing 6–8 inches from the fold to 4–6 inches from the bottom edge to sew the side seams (the long sides). You can always make the armhole opening bigger or smaller depending on how it feels when you try it on.

2. Reinforce the shoulder ends of the boatneck opening by sewing a bar tack at each end.

3. Press all the seams open.

4. Finish the neck edge, the armhole edges, the hem, and the side slits with a very tiny double-fold hem or any of the other hems and finishes suggested in chapters 2 and 7.

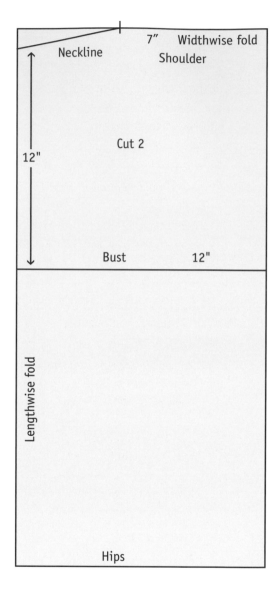

Fabric with Nap

MATERIALS

- 2 lengths of a soft fabric. (A length of fabric is from your shoulders to somewhere between your hips and waist, depending on how long you want the top to be.)

NOTE: If the fabric is 60 inches wide and you are small, you might need only one length.

- Matching thread
- A yardstick
- Your waist (W) and bust (B) measurements
- The length (L) you want the top to be

CUT THE FABRIC AND CREATE THE NECK OPENING

1. Cut two rectangles 3 or 4 inches (depending on how much ease you want) wider than half of your hip or bust measurement, whichever is larger, and the length from your neck to where you want the bottom edge of the top to be.

2. With right sides together, fold the squares together widthwise and mark the center point on the fold. The tops should be in the same direction on both pieces.

3. Unfold the fabric and start stitching the shoulder seams about 4 inches from this center point to the outer edge. Try it on. If it goes over your head, reinforce the seam at the neck edge. If it doesn't, remove a few stitches at a time in both directions. Stop when you can easily fit your head through the hole. Reinforce the stitching at the neck edge of the seam by sewing a bar tack at each end of the neck opening.

ASSEMBLE THE NAP BOATNECK TOP

1. With right sides together, measuring from the shoulder seam, begin sewing about 6–8 inches from the seam to about 4–6 inches from the bottom edge to sew the side seams. Measuring from the shoulder seam, begin sewing about 6–8 inches from the seam to about 4–6 inches from the bottom edge. You can always make the armhole opening bigger or smaller depending on how it feels when you try it on.

2. Press all seams open.

3. Finish the neck edge, the armhole edges, the hem, and the side slits with a very tiny double-fold hem or any of the other hem and finishing suggestions earlier in this chapter or in Chapter 5.

Variations

TIE BELT

Add a tie belt on the front. Put a casing on the inside front anywhere between your waist and bust. You can start at the side seams or any distance from the side seams. Sew one or two buttonholes on the center front line of the casing. Thread ties through the casing, stitching the end of the casing and tie together at the side seam or wherever it began. Pull ties through buttonholes and tie with a bow in the front. (See Chapter 2 for tie belts and casings.)

SCOOP NECK

Make the boatneck with about a ½- to 2-inch scoop. When the fabric is folded in quarters and you have marked the center point, cut a slight curve, with the lowest point on the center fold. The cut at the shoulder and center front lines should be at right angles to the folds. When finishing the neck edge, use single-fold or double-fold bias tape.

SHOULDER STRAPS

Make two ¼- to ½-inch straps about 10 inches long. (See Chapter 2 for making straps.) Stitching in the middle of the strap, sew the strap to the middle of the inside of the shoulder seam. Pull the ends to the outside and tie the shoulder seam with a bow. You can also include your bra strap in with the tie.

This loose-fitting halter top is easy to make. Because it has a lined top, you don't have to worry about facings or finishing neck and armhole edges. All dimensions are approximate because, with an elastic back and tie front, the top doesn't have to fit you exactly.

Make the Summer Top

MATERIALS

NOTE: Make the pattern and muslin mock-up first before buying your fabric. Then you will be able to purchase exactly what you need.

- 1–1½ yards of fabric, depending on how long you want the top to be

- The same amount of lightweight lining

- ½-inch elastic

- Ribbon for neck (if you aren't making a tie of the same fabric)

- Thread to match

MAKE THE PATTERN

There are two pattern pieces to this top, a front and a back, and both are placed on the fold. You will use these pattern pieces for the lining as well.

Before making your garment, make a muslin mock-up. Adjust the pattern pieces to suit your body shape and taste.

FRONT

1 Measure your bust (B), waist (W), hips (H), and the length (L) from about 2 inches under your chin to where you want the hem of the top to be.

2 The center front line will be the edge of your paper and is L plus 1 inch for ½-inch seam allowances. Mark on your paper pattern that the center front line will be placed on the fold of the fabric. Draw a line perpendicular to the center front fold line about 2 inches above the top of L.

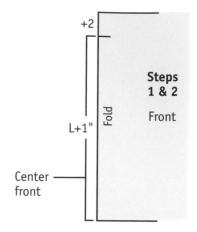

3 On this line, measure over about 5 inches for small or 7 inches for large, and place a mark S for the shoulder. Draw a slight scoopneck line from the top of the original L mark to S.

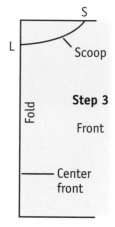

4 About 6 inches down from the top of L, draw another line perpendicular to the fold line. Divide your B measurement by 4, and add 2–5 inches for ease and ½ inch for seam allowance for the length of this line (BL).

5 On end of this horizontal line BL inches made in step 4, put a mark A. This should be the approximation of the bottom or the armhole. Draw a diagonal line from S to A. Round off in a curve at the bottom to form the base of the armhole.

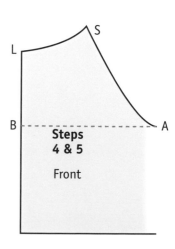

6 At the bottom of L, draw a horizontal line approximately one-quarter of your hip measurement plus a 2–4 inch ease allowance and $\frac{1}{2}$-inch seam allowance (H).

7 Draw a line from A to H for the side seam. This completes the front pattern piece.

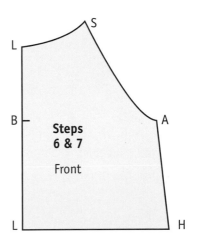

BACK

1 For the back of the top pattern, draw a quadrilateral beginning with a vertical fold line. The length (L) of this fold line is the length of the side front established from A to H on the front pattern.

2 Draw a horizontal line from A perpendicular to the fold equal to one-quarter of your bust measurement plus 2–4 inches of ease and $\frac{1}{2}$-inch seam allowance.

3 Draw a horizontal line from the bottom of L perpendicular to the fold, one-quarter of your hip measurement plus $\frac{1}{2}$-inch seam allowance and 2–4 inches of ease.

4 Connect the ends of the right edge to form the back pattern.

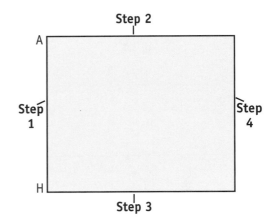

Cut It Out and Put It Together

1 Cut both the front and back pieces on the fold. Cut out the lining in the same way, except make the front and back lining pieces ½ inch shorter.

2 With right sides together, sew the side seams of the garment together. Repeat with the lining side seams.

3 With right sides together, sew the lining to the garment along the top of the back, around the armholes, and across the top of the front. Clip the curves and press the seam allowances toward the lining. Understitch as desired. Trim the corners (see Chapter 2).

4 Turn the garment right side out. Press the edges flat.

5 Topstitch a ½- to 1-inch casing across the top of the back. (See Chapter 6 for casings.)

6 Topstitch a ½- to 1-inch casing across the top of the front neck.

7 Carefully unstitch (rip out) a few stitches in the seam at the two sides of the casing on the front to allow room for insertion of the ties.

8 Carefully unstitch (rip out) a few stitches on the inside of the lining side seams of the casing on either side of the back to allow room for insertion of the elastic.

9 Insert elastic into back casing. Secure both ends by stitching in the ditch. Hand stitch the seam openings closed (see Chapter 2).

10 Hem the lining and the garment with ¼-inch double-fold hem (see Chapter 5). Check to make sure the lining does not hang below the garment. Tack the lining to the garment in the side seam allowance (see Chapter 2).

11 Make a tie approximately 60 inches long and 1½–2 inches wide from contrasting fabric or ribbon. (See Chapter 2 for making ties.)

12 Thread the tie through the front casing.

Tank tops are very easy to make. A tank top usually has a scoop neck on both the front and the back, but does not have sleeves. Most tank top patterns consist of two pieces, a front and a back, and possibly neck and armhole facings or bias strip finishing.

You can make tank tops from stretchy or nonstretchy fabrics.

- If you choose jersey or some other knit, the neckline and armhole are usually finished with a strip made from the same fabric or with purchased matching or contrasting rib-knit trim.

- If you choose a lightweight woven fabric, the neckline and armholes are usually finished with one facing that includes the armholes and the neck, or you may use purchased double-fold bias tape or make your own. (See the section on one-piece neck and armhole facings in Chapter 7.)

- If you choose a heavy woven fabric, the neckline and armholes are usually finished with a one-piece facing of a lightweight fabric or lining fabric. It's also possible to finish the neckline and armholes differently using the suggestions from Chapter 7.

MATERIALS

- ⅞ yards of 60-inch or 1¼ yards of 44-inch fabric makes a size 10. If you wear a larger or smaller size, you will need more or less fabric.

- Double-fold bias tape, matching or contrasting (optional)

- Matching thread

DESIGN YOUR TANK TOP

You have some decisions to make before you begin:

- What kind of fabric do you want to use?

- How wide do you want the shoulder straps to be?

- How much scoop do you want in the front and back neckline?

- How long do you want the top to be?

- How much ease do you want?

As with all garments you make without a purchased pattern, first create a paper pattern using the suggested pattern on the right as a beginning. Don't be afraid to change the width of the straps, the amount of scoop on the neck, the length, or the width to suit your body and your tastes.

Depending on the type of fabric you are using for your tank top, choose either the pattern for stretchy fabric or the one for nonstretchy fabric.

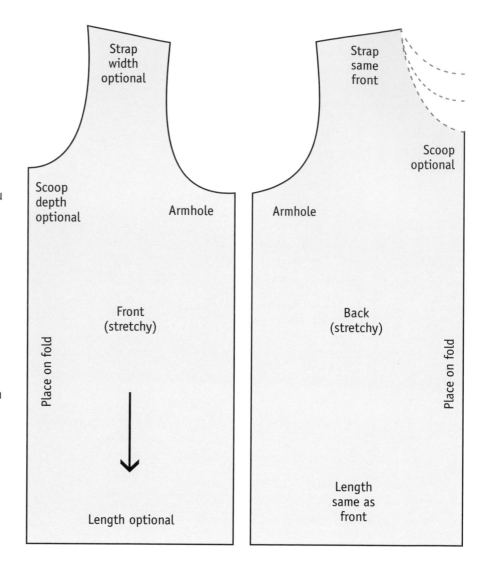

Remember the width of each pattern piece through the bust area should be one-fourth your bust measurement plus 2–4 inches ease. Likewise, the width of the lower edge of each piece should be one-fourth your hip measurement plus 2–4 inches ease.

NOTE: The nonstretchy fabric has a bust dart. If you're using this pattern, you may have to move the point of the dart up or down so that the dart points to your bust. (For more on bust darts, see the section on darts earlier in this chapter and in Chapter 2.)

CUT OUT AND ASSEMBLE THE TANK TOP

1 Cut out both the front and back pieces.

2 If you have chosen bust darts, sew them in first.

3 Sew the back and front shoulder seams together.

4 Sew the back and front side seams together.

5 Hem the bottom edge.

6 If you are using double-fold bias tape, finish the neck and armholes.

If you are not using double-fold bias tape, cut some bias strips from the fabric. Fold the fabric in half lengthwise and press. Fold the edges to the inside. (It should resemble purchased double-fold bias tape.) Sew the newly made bias strips to the armholes and the neck opening.

NOTE: If you are using a stretchy fabric, you do not need to cut these strips on the bias.

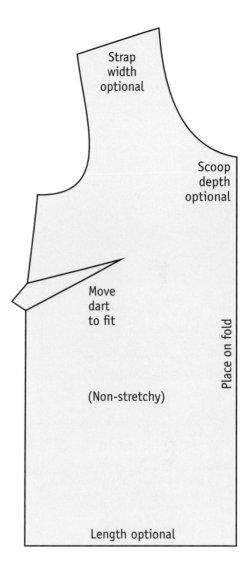

225

CHAPTER 11

Dresses

A dress is simply a top and a skirt in one garment. In terms of design, the sky's the limit. Hemlines are anywhere, waistlines are everywhere, and styles of necklines are almost infinite. Historically, if you look through fashion books, you could almost date the fashion, at least within the decade, if not the year, by the hemline, waistline location, or neckline style. Today, the rules older generations of sewers learned in home economics classes or from their mothers and grandmothers no longer apply. Fabrics have changed, sewing machines have changed, color combinations have changed, and design is up to the sewer's creativity.

In this chapter are some simple dresses. Remember that these are only a jumping-off point for your imagination.

Dress Styles

oyday, while functional, dress styles are about fashion and creativity. The following are four basic dress styles. By varying the fabric, the length and neckline, each of these styles can be the basis for any garment from simple to fancy, from lounging around the house to going out on the town.

SHEATH

As the name suggests, a sheath dress is a covering, as a knife sheath is a covering for a knife. The silhouette is the same as the silhouette of the female body with a slight indentation for the waist. The sheath is not as tight as a garment made from spandex. There is both a small amount of design and a small amount of wearing ease. The fabric lays on the body smoothly without pulling and wrinkling. In the middle of the twentieth century, most of the shaping was accomplished with darts: bust, waist, and derriere. Women encouraged their bodies into hour glass shapes with girdles. In general, the twenty-first century has encouraged more free flowing styles—fewer darts and more wearing ease. The same pattern of a sheath dress can be appropriate for an afternoon picnic or a night on the town by just changing the fabric from cotton to velvet for example. In this chapter you will find a simple pattern for a sheath dress, and most pattern companies also have some basic sheath dress patterns.

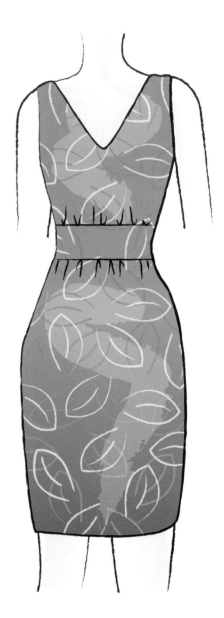

CLASSIC SHIRT DRESS

When you think of a shirt dress, think of a long shirt. Some shirt dresses, formerly called shirtwaist dresses, had a skirt attached to the bodice/shirt/blouse/top at the waistline. Shirt dresses are characterized by a looseness of fit and buttons down the front. They may have sleeves of any length or no sleeves. They may have collars of any kind or no collar. For the most part, the bodice of a shirt dress is a shirt (or blouse). There are usually no zippers, because the dress is put on like a coat with buttons down the front. In the fashion of the early twenty-first century, you may want to eliminate the waist-line seam and make the top and bottom all of one piece. Most pattern companies have patterns for some classic shirt waist dresses.

PRINCESS LINE

One of the most enduring designs for women's fashion involves "the princess line." Princess lines on tops or dresses are very flattering to many women. They are often found on evening wear or fancy dresses. All the shaping takes place in the seam lines. There are very few, if any, darts. There is usually no waist seam. The skirt can be straight, A-line, or flared. The princess-line has two side seams, two front seams, and three back seams. The front princess lines start at the shoulder or in the armhole (unless the dress is strapless), go over the fullest part of the bust, and continue to the hem. The two back princess seams start at the same place on the shoulder or armhole as the front seams, go over the shoulder blade bone or just below it, and continue to the hem. If there is a back zipper, there will also be a center-back seam. If the opening is in the front, there will be a front-center seam.

WRAPAROUND

A wraparound dress is just that, a dress that wraps around the body. It is similar to a wraparound skirt with a wrap top attached. Think of a big wraparound bathrobe with a bit more design. Often the front piece that overlaps has a ruffle or is shaped with curve on the overlapping edge and bottom. Wraparound dresses usually wrap to the left side of the front.

All dresses have certain design elements in common to consider. They all have bottoms, tradition-ally called hems. They all must accommodate your shape—bust, derriere, hips, and waist. They all have various types of necklines, backs, and sleeves—or no sleeves at all. Finally, all dresses must have a way for their wearer to get into and out of them! All the possibilities suggested for skirts and tops in the prior chapters can be combined into a dress.

WAISTLINES

Some dresses have defined waistlines that sit at your actual waist. Other dresses do not have an identified waistline at all. On still others, the horizontal "waistline" is anywhere from near the hemline to above the bust line. When this line is just under the bust, for example, it is referred to as an *empire waist*. When the horizontal line is below your true waistline, it is called a *drop waist*.

SKIRTS

The skirts on dresses vary from straight to full flare. The skirt and bodice pieces can be assembled separately and then sewn together at the designated waistline, or the skirt and bodice can be cut as one piece without a waist-line seam, eliminating any horizontal line feature.

HEMLINES

As with skirts, dress hemlines can be anywhere from the floor to the top of the thighs. The hemline can be parallel to the floor, at an angle, or at many angles.

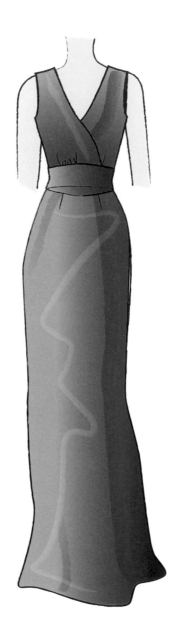

BODICES

You can turn almost any top into a dress by lengthening it or by adding a skirt. Make almost any dress a top just by cutting off the skirt. The bodice features are the same in both cases. The shaping features include the bust, shoulder blade and waist darts, tucks, and gathers. The fashion features include the shape of the neckline, the type of sleeve treatment or no sleeve, and where and how the bodice attaches to the skirt.

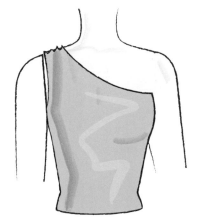  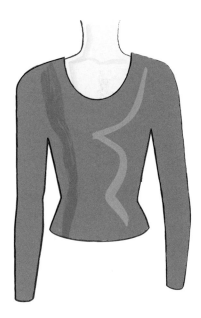

SLEEVES

The design and insertion of sleeves are basically the same for dresses as they are for tops (see the section on sleeves in Chapter 9). The bodice may be sleeveless or just have straps of a variety of widths. Sleeves could also be asymmetrical, having one shoulder/arm covered by a sleeve/strap and the other shoulder/arm strapless and sleeveless.

If you like to lounge around in comfortable dresses, try this easy-to-make dress. All you need are three rectangles if the fabric does not have a nap, four rectangles if it does. See Chapter 1 for a definition of nap. You can add two more small rectangles for patch pockets if you like or two more rectangles for sleeves.

Three-Rectangle Dress

MATERIALS

The amount of fabric you need is determined by the width of the fabric and how long and full you want the skirt and the size and shape of your body.

Using steps 1 and 2 below, calculate how much fabric you will need.

- **Step 1:** Approximately 2 yards of 45-inch or 1 yard of 60-inch fabric with a soft drape for the skirt
- **Step 2:** Approximately 1 yard of 45-inch or 60-inch fabric with a soft drape for the top

NOTE: The skirt and top can be cut from the same fabric or the top could be a coordinating fabric.

- Thread to match or contrast with the fabric
- 1 package medium wide double-fold bias tape to match or contrast with the fabric

PRE-ASSEMBLY OF THE THREE-RECTANGLE DRESS

① Prepare the fabric as described in Chapter 2 by shrinking and pressing as appropriate for the type of fabric. Determine the width and length needed as described on next page and cut Rectangle 1 from your chosen fabric. This rectangle will form the top (front and back) of your dress.

The width of Rectangle 1 (shoulder to shoulder) depends on how long you want the two sleeves to be.

The sleeve length can be from slightly extended sleeves, as shown in the photo on previous page, to long sleeves depending on the look that you want, your size, and the width of your fabric.

The length of Rectangle 1 is 2 times the distance from the top of your shoulder near the neckline to where you want the horizontal line (waistline) to be. The horizontal seam line that attaches the top to the skirt can be just under the bust, at your waistline, near your hips, or anywhere in between. The horizontal line width needs to be wide enough to go over your shoulders and bust.

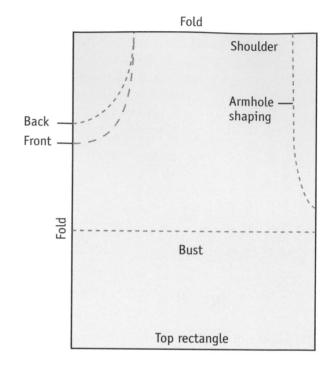

② Fold the rectangle in half so that the fold line (width) of the fabric will be faux shoulder seams with half of the rectangle forming the front of the top and the other half forming the back of the top.

Fold on lengthwise grain to mark neckline. Choose one of the necklines described in Chapter 7. The dress shown here has a slight scoop in the back and a slightly deeper scoop in the front.

NOTE: Remember to start small and work to a larger neckline. Increase the neckhole size by very small increments. See Chapter 10 under "Make a Boatneck Top" for more complete measurements and increments. It is easier to start with a small hole and increase it than it is to start with a large hole and decrease it!

NOTE: If the fabric you have chosen for the top has a nap or directional pattern, see note after Step 7 before continuing.

③ Cut rectangles 2 and 3 from your chosen fabric. These two rectangles will form the skirt of your dress. Make them the length you want the dress to be from the location of the horizontal seam line in Step 1 plus ⅝ inches for the waist seam and the extra amount you need for the hem allowance, which will depend on the type of hem you choose from Chapter 5. The width of rectangles should be several inches (at least 4 inches for ease) wider than your hip measurement, depending on how much ease and/or fullness you want. These rectangles will be the back and front skirt part of the dress. See Chapter 4 for more information on ease.

ASSEMBLY OF THE THREE-RECTANGLE DRESS

① Following the directions in Chapter 7, finish the armholes and neckhole. In the dress shown here, the armholes were finished with a simple small double-fold hem, and the neckhole was finished with matching medium-wide double-fold bias tape. See Chapter 7 for more information on neckline and armhole finishes.

② Sew the side seams together, including the underarm seams of any extended sleeves. Clip the curve where the side seam curves into the sleeve as needed to eliminate puckering and pulling of the fabric.

③ Sew the side seams of rectangles 2 and 3 together to form the skirt. Sew a gathering stitch around the top edge. See Chapter 2 for how to gather.

NOTE: You may want pleats or darts instead of gathers (see Chapter 2 for directions).

④ Attach the skirt to the top by sewing a standard seam with right sides together, matching the side seams and front and back midpoints and adjusting the gathers of the skirt to fit the top as necessary so that the fullness is evenly distributed. Finish the hem with one of the methods described in Chapter 5.

NOTE: If the fabric you have chosen for the top rectangle has a nap or a printed design with a definite up and down pattern, you will have to cut rectangle 1 in half at the shoulder fold line and turn one piece upside down and sew the rectangle back together at what now becomes shoulder seams.

See page 258 in Chapter 6 if you want to put elastic around the waist similar to the photo above.

A Sheath Dress

This straight dress has two main pieces: the front and the back. Both pieces are cut on the lengthwise grain. The front piece is placed on the fold. The back is cut in two pieces to accommodate a zipper. Sleeves are optional, but if you do use them, save set-in sleeves until after you have gained some dressmaking experience. If you choose to finish the neck and armhole with facings, you will also need a neck facing and an armhole facing. The neckline may be of any design, but a round or scoop neck is the easiest for a beginning sewer; do not start with a keyhole or other complicated neckline or with a collar.

Construct the Sheath Dress

MATERIALS

- 1 or 2 (depending on your size and width of the fabric) lengths of fabric (a length is from your chin to where you want the hem to be, plus enough fabric for the fold-up hem allowance.)

- 22-inch dress zipper
- Thread to match fabric

PRE-ASSEMBLY OF THE SHEATH DRESS

1 Make a paper copy of the pattern shown on the following page. This pattern is only a suggestion of the basic shape of the pieces. You will have to put in your measurements where indicated and add the seam allowance to each pattern piece.

② Make a muslin mock-up of the dress without facings or zipper as described in Chapter 4.

③ Try on and make any necessary adjustments to the pattern for proper fit. Adjust the facings the same way. See Chapter 4, "Finding the Right Fit." You may have to add some bust or shoulder darts.

④ Prepare and press the fabric. Lay out, cut, and mark it. See chapters 1 and 3 for more information on preparing, laying out, and cutting fabric. See Chapter 7 for cutting facings.

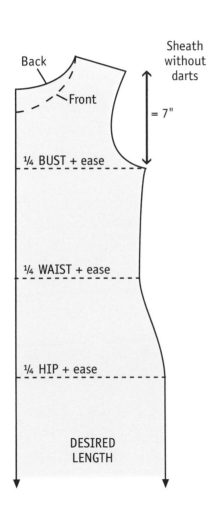

Sheath without darts

Back
Front
= 7"
¼ BUST + ease
¼ WAIST + ease
¼ HIP + ease
DESIRED LENGTH

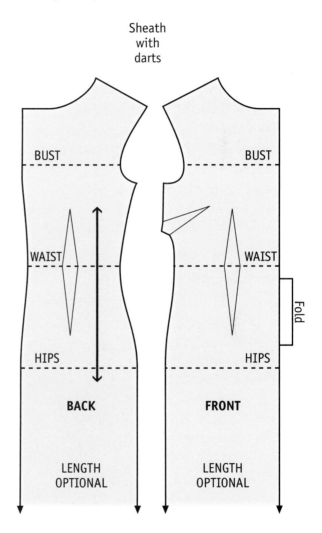

Sheath with darts

BUST
WAIST
HIPS
BACK
LENGTH OPTIONAL

BUST
WAIST
Fold
HIPS
FRONT
LENGTH OPTIONAL

ASSEMBLY OF THE SHEATH DRESS

The basic steps for assembling this dress are few and simple:

1 If you have added darts, stitch darts in the front and back sections.

2 Stay-stitch all edges of a woven fabric that might ravel but particularly the neck edges of all fabrics to prevent stretching. See Chapter 2 for stay-stitching directions.

3 Put the zipper in the center-back seam (see Chapter 2). Finish the back seam.

4 Stitch the front section and the back section right sides together at the shoulder seams using the standard ⅝ inches for seams.

5 Interface the neck facings and seam the front and back facings together. Press the seams open. Sew on neck facing and armhole facings by placing them right sides together on the respective areas of the dress. Under-stitch facings. See chapters 2 and 9.

6 Sew the side seams together.

7 Finish the hem (see Chapter 5).

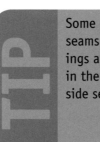

TIP

Some patterns suggest sewing the side seams together before putting in the facings and/or the sleeves. It is easier to put in the sleeve or facing before sewing the side seams together in most cases.

A Peasant Dress

The peasant dress, that staple of the '60s and '70s, has made a comeback in recent years. While still retaining elements of its folk and hippy free-and-easy heritage (such as embroidery around the neckline, and puffed sleeves, to name two), the peasant dress can transition from casual to the workplace to evening by layering on a jacket, vest, or sweater. Peasant dresses go well with leggings, jeans, or bare legs underneath.

Construct the Peasant Dress

MATERIALS

- 2 lengths of bodice fabric (a length is from your chin to where you want the hem to be, plus enough fabric for the fold-up hem allowance) plus 2 lengths of sleeve fabric (a length is from the base of your neckline to where you want the hem to be, plus enough fabric for the fold-up hem allowance or casing)
- ¼-inch wide elastic
- Single-fold bias tape (for options with waist or upper arm casings)
- Thread to match fabric

PRE-ASSEMBLY

① Make paper copies of the patterns shown in the diagram on the next page. This pattern is only a suggestion of the basic shape of the pieces. You will have to put in your measurements where indicated and add the seam allowance to each pattern piece.

② Prepare and press the fabric. Lay out, cut, and mark it. See chapters 1 and 3 for more information on preparing, laying out, and cutting fabric.

ASSEMBLY

The basic steps for assembling this dress are as follows:

① Stitch the sleeve pieces to the bodice pieces, right sides together, using a standard ⅝-inch seam allowance. Trim and finish the seam allowances.

② Press the seam allowances to the side so that they are all pointing in the same direction.

③ Edge finish the top neckline edge. Fold the top edge over 1 inch to form the casing (see Chapter 2).

④ Stitch ⅜ inches from the folded edge, leaving a 1-inch opening in the center back.

⑤ Insert the desired length of elastic into the neckline casing through the opening. Stitch the ends of the elastic together, and stitch the opening closed.

⑥ Arrange the garment so that the right sides of the bodice front and back pieces are facing. Align the sleeve and side edges.

⑦ Stitch the sleeve and side seams. Edge finish the seam allowances.

⑧ Repeat steps 2–5 for the sleeve openings.

⑨ Add a bias tape casing at the desired waistline position and insert elastic (see chapters 2 and 6).

⑩ Finish the hem (see Chapter 5).

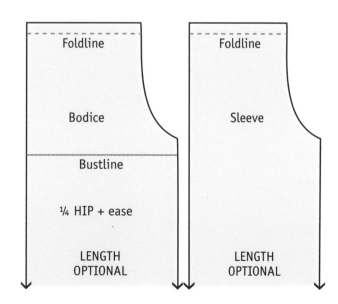

CHAPTER 12

Recycle, Refurbish, and Repair

We all have garments in our closets that we can't bear to throw out but haven't worn for years. Now is the time to apply the three "Rs"— recycle, refurbish, and repair—to some of those perfectly good but possibly outdated clothes. Use your sewing skills to remake or re-design a garment into something to wear and enjoy!

Moreover, you can make your garments last longer and look bet-ter, repairing so invisibly that no one will ever know it was mended, or repairing in such a way that the fix becomes an embellishment and enhances your fashion statement. In this chapter are some quick solu-tions that in some cases take only minutes to accomplish, plus a few that may take more time and concentration.

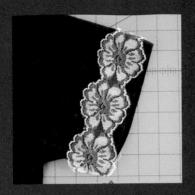

Make Over Your Denim

Have your favorite jeans or denim skirt seen better days, but you can't bring yourself to throw them out? Don't worry! Give them new life with godets or some trim or embellishment. Perhaps you could add a flannel lining, turn wide-leg jeans into slim-leg jeans, or transform full-length jeans into capris with side slits.

If you don't have any old jeans, you can shop at thrift stores or garage sales for good buys on jeans. Even if they don't exactly fit you, you can use them for parts of other designs.

Add Godets

Godets are fabric pieces (typically triangles with rounded bottoms) inserted into a seam. They add flare and fashion to your jeans or jean skirts.

2

1. Find some lightweight funky fabric. You don't need much for two godets; look for fabric-store remnants or in your own stash. Think about the fabric's drape and how the godet will appear.

2. Decide how far up the seam from the hem bottom— and how wide at the bottom—you want the godet to be, and then mark it.

3. Make two godets the size you want, plus seam allowance. There is no rule about what size to make them— experiment until you find the size that you like.

NOTE: Try making one approximately 6 inches high and 3 inches wide to see if it works for your taste.

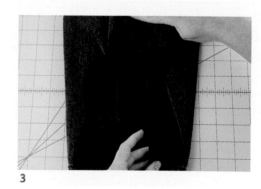

3

Another part of the godet to experiment with is the shape of the bottom. It can be rounded, straight, or even have a point.

4. Use a hem stitch of your choice to hem the godet (see Chapter 5 for more on hems).

5 Slit the side seams of the jeans ½ inch shorter than the height of the godet. Trim off any extra bulk from the seam. Most jeans have flat-felled seams, so it's easier to cut two slits—one on each side of the seam. (*Flat-felled seams* are machine-stitched in a way that encloses the raw edges. These seams are very strong.)

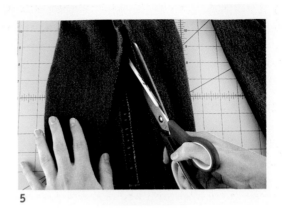

5

6 With right sides together, pin one side of the godet to the jeans, starting at the hem. Match up the hem of the godet with the hem of the pants. Adjust the top of the point as needed.

NOTE: This is not an exact science. Stitch a ¼-inch seam as far up to the point as you can get.

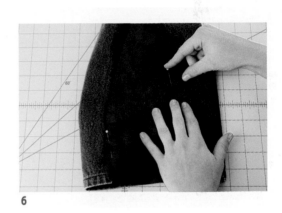

6

7 When you get to the top of the point, you may have trouble sewing over the thickness of the jean seam. Don't worry. Stop and pin the other side of the godet, right sides together, to the other side of the jeans, again matching the godet hem and the jeans hem. Sew the other side from the hem to the point with a ¼-inch seam allowance. Finish the point with a few stitches of hand sewing if necessary.

7

Make a Jean Skirt

You can make this skirt any length you want.

① Undo the inside leg seam of a pair of jeans. It's easier to cut on either side of the seam than it is to try to take out all the stitches.

② Cut off the crotch points so that the leg opening makes a smooth V.

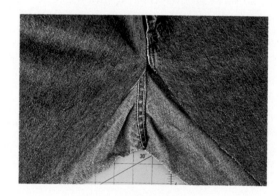

③ From another pair of jeans or some other fabric, make two large godets the size of the V leg opening plus seam allowance for both the front and back of the skirt.

NOTE: The front and back godets do not need to be made of the same fabric (see "Add Godets," earlier in this chapter). Trim the bottom of the godet with a small curve and hem.

④ Pin and sew the godet to the skirt. See Step 7 of "Add Godets," earlier in this chapter, for inserting the godet into the skirt.

NOTE: If you want a funkier look, you can sew the godet right side to the jean wrong side so that the jean edge will fray slightly.

⑤ Trim the hem to the length you want all the way around and then hem following one of the suggestions in Chapter 2.

NOTE: You will have to use your judgment about how much curve you want on the bottom of the skirt. It will depend somewhat on how wide the godet is at the hem edge.

Embellish Your Jeans

APPLIQUÉS

A wide variety of appliqués are available at fabric stores. They can be sewn on, ironed on, or glued on. If you choose to glue, use reliable washable fabric glue. Test the glue before using it on your finished garment. Make sure it doesn't come undone in the washer. Or you can slip-stitch the appliqués to your jeans by hand. If they're in an easy place to reach with the sewing machine, zig-zag the edge in place.

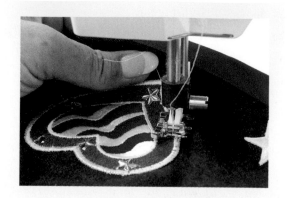

TRIM OR BRAID

Trim and braid can be functional as well as decorative. If your jeans are a little tight through the hips and leg, slit down the outside seam, remove the seam allowance, and add a strip of decorative fabric, braid, or trim the width you need plus seam allowances. If your jeans fit and you don't need any additional width, then just topstitch a braid or trim right beside the outside seam. You can also stitch trim or braid around each leg just above the hem to give your jeans an updated look.

EMBROIDERY

You can embroider by hand or with a sewing machine programmed with embroidery stitches. Many easy embroidery stitches for hand sewing are available in how-to books and online. To embellish your back pockets, carefully rip out the stitches that hold them onto the jeans, and then embroider a design on the pockets; then resew the pockets onto your jeans with a topstitch.

You may have trouble machine-embroidering down a narrow leg or near the hem because of seam thickness. Rip out (or cut out entirely) the lower leg inseam so that it lies flat, machine-embroider, and then resew the seam using an ordinary ½-inch straight seam. Doing so will make the jeans smaller around the legs.

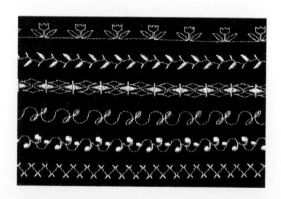

Almost everyone has extra T-shirts lying around. Instead of turning them into rags, try the alterations in this section to fashion brand-new, stylish garments.

Reshape the Waist

Many T-shirts have very little shaping. If your body shape has a narrower waist, you will look better by reshaping your T-shirts to mimic your body shape. Give your favorite tee some flattering new curves by nipping in the waist. Here's how:

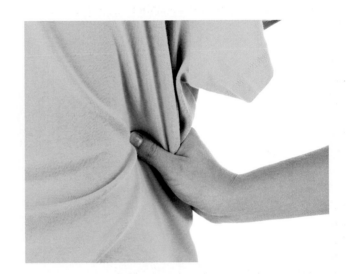

① Try on your T-shirt and, using your fingers, pinch in a fold at the waist of approximately the amount you need to make the T-shirt look better on you. Measure and note this amount.

Take off the T-shirt and turn it inside out.

② Lay the T-shirt on a flat surface with the side seams smooth. Draw a smooth curve from the underarm in to the waist the approximate amount you pinched out and then back out to the hem on the side seams, indenting where your waist will be. Be sure both sides of the shirt are equal, with the same shaping.

③ Pin the seams along these lines and try on the T-shirt, still inside out.

④ Adjust the pins to create more or less curve as needed. When you have the shape you want, re-mark the line according to where you had it pinned and stitch the side seams, following along the new marked line (see Chapter 1 for marking tools).

⑤ Trim the excess fabric in the seam allowance from the seams.

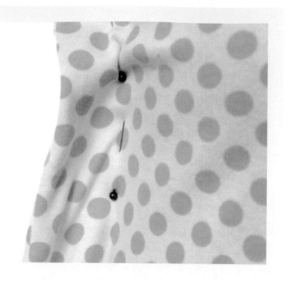

Redo the Sleeves

If the T-shirt has a regular set-in sleeve, remove the original sleeves and replace them with binding, trim, lace, or embroidery.

You can also easily convert a set-in sleeve to another style such as a cap sleeve. For a cap sleeve, just cut the old sleeve by removing the underarm seam and curving the sleeve opening, shortening to a length that pleases you.

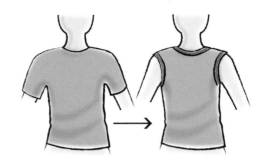

Leave the sleeves in place. Remove the ribbon band and replace with a band of fabric, woven or knit of another color and width. Before cutting the band of woven fabric, be sure it will easily go over your hand and arm. Put on the new band as if it were a waistband (see Chapter 6).

You can also add embroidery, trim, or lace to the hem of a sleeve as shown at right.

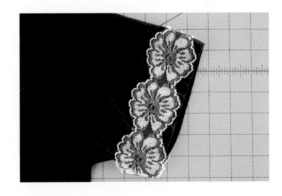

Find two T-shirts with long sleeves. The colors should be different but coordinating. Cut off the sleeves on both shirts at the same length. Swap the sleeves to the other shirt and resew with a narrow hem. The length is up to you. If you're feeling adventurous, do not cut the sleeves straight across, but with some angle or irregular shape. Just be sure to cut the sleeves on both shirts exactly the same.

Convert a T-Shirt into a Dress

Because T-shirts are so flexible, they make great tops for slip-on dresses with no zippers—terrific for the beach or to hang out around the house. To make a T-shirt dress, you will need a T-shirt and some fabric for a skirt. How much fabric you need depends on how long and how full you want the skirt to be. To estimate how much fabric you'll need, hold the fabric up to you. A yard might be enough if you want a shorter tunic; use 2 yards if you want the dress to be longer. You will be making two rectangles of equal size.

1 Decide where you want the waistline to be. It could be just under your bust (empire style), at your waist, or between your waist and hip line (drop-waist style).

2 Decide where you want the hem of the skirt to be—mini, knee length, mid-calf, and so on (see Chapter 5 on lengths).

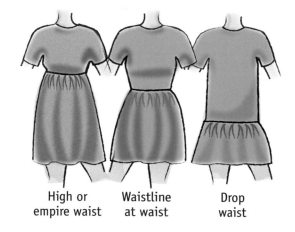

High or empire waist   Waistline at waist   Drop waist

3 The difference between where you decided to put the waistline in Step 1 and the overall dress length plus a hem allowance will determine the length of the two rectangles you will cut to create the skirt. Each rectangle will be at least 4 inches wider than your hips and preferably as wide as the bottom edge of the T-shirt.

NOTE: Don't forget to add seam allowances for the strips to be sewn onto the T-shirt and a hem allowance for the fabric skirt.

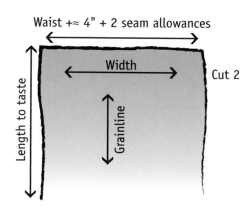

Waist +≈ 4" + 2 seam allowances

Width

Cut 2

Length to taste

Grainline

4   Sew the side seams of the skirt together and finish the hem (see Chapter 5 on hems).

5   At the top edge of the skirt, sew two gathering lines of stitches. Gently gather the skirt along the gathering lines (see Chapter 2).

6   Cut the T-shirt where you want the skirt to begin; remember to leave about ½ to ⅝ inches of extra length for the seam allowance where the skirt will be sewn onto the T-shirt.

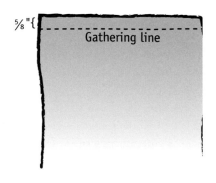

⅝"{ Gathering line

7   Pin the gathered skirt to the bottom of the cut-off T-shirt, right sides together, stretching the T-shirt gently as you pin. If it's too tight, it won't fit over your shoulders and bust. Try to keep the gathers of the skirt evenly distributed by matching side seams and center front and back points (see Chapter 5).

8   Sew the skirt to the T-shirt by stitching on top of the gathering stitching. Continue to gently ease the tee to the skirt as you stitch (see Chapter 5). You want the T-shirt edge to be the same length as the gathered skirt edge. The T-shirt edge has a great deal of stretch. If it's stretched too much, it won't spring back to its original size after it is sewn to the skirt. With a little practice, you will be able to "ease" the T-shirt fabric to the skirt fabric just the right amount.

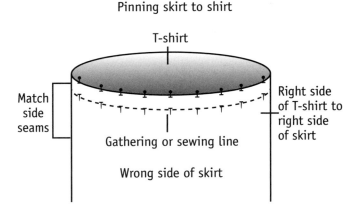

Pinning skirt to shirt

T-shirt

Match side seams

Right side of T-shirt to right side of skirt

Gathering or sewing line

Wrong side of skirt

9 Try on the dress. If you can't get it over your head, loosen the stitches that attach the skirt to the top by breaking the thread in a few places, spreading out the gathers, and restitching the skirt to the top.

10 Trim the seam allowance.

11 Sew an elastic casing (see Chapter 2 on casings) over the seam allowance on the wrong side of the garment. The bottom line of stitching goes in the ditch of the waist seam (see Chapter 2 for stitching in the ditch). The bobbin stitches of the line sewing the top edge of the casing will show on the right side like topstitching, so plan the color of your bobbin thread accordingly. Again, stretch the T-shirt gently as you sew on the casing.

12 Measure a piece of elastic to fit gently around your chosen waist/hip location. Thread the elastic through the casing and sew the ends together (see Chapter 2).

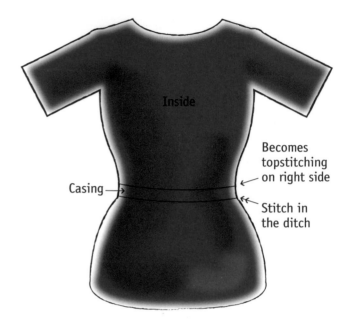

Inside

Becomes topstitching on right side

Casing

Stitch in the ditch

Updating or changing a skirt is both easy and fun. It's also a great opportunity to show off your creative talents. In this section I will show you how to change the length as well as the style of a skirt—for example, changing an A-line skirt to a pencil or straight skirt.

From Long to Short

The simplest way to shorten a long straight skirt or slightly A-line skirt is to cut off the bottom and rehem. Save the cut-off piece; it may come in handy someday! You may use it for a patch pocket, for a scarf, or to mend a small tear later.

1 Decide where you want the new hem of the skirt to be by pinning up the hem and trying on the skirt to see if the new length flatters you.

2 Take off the skirt and mark the fold line by putting pins right in the folded edge. Leaving the pins in the folded edge, unpin the hem. Unpin the folded edge.

This pinned line is the new finished length of the skirt. To this measurement, add the hem allowance that will be turned up (usually 1 to 2 inches). This finished length plus the hem allowance is the cutting line.

1

3 Mark this cutting line with pins or a marking pencil (see Chapter 1 for marking tools). If you aren't shortening the skirt very much, you may need to rip out the original hem allowance before cutting off the skirt.

4 Cut the excess fabric from the skirt.

5 Hem the skirt (see Chapter 5).

3

From Short to Long

Years ago, letting down the hem was the standard method to lengthen a skirt. Today, most manufactured skirts have very little hem to let down. If you want just a little more length, do the following:

1. Rip out the existing hem and topstitch a hem binding to the skirt bottom edge, with the wrong side of the binding to the right side of the garment.

2. Fold and press the hem binding to the inside of the garment. If you need an even narrower hem, you can use the binding itself as the hem allowance and topstitch the other edge of it in place. Alternatively, sew the top of the binding to the garment by hand, using the catch stitch. (See Chapter 5 for more details on hemming.)

TIP

The crease line of an existing hem is often difficult to press out and is, in some cases, very visible when the hem is undone. You can put a decorative stitch right on top of the hem crease or topstitch a trim or braid over it to hide the crease if it won't press out. Sometimes it's better to cut it off completely and try something new.

Changing an A-Line to a Straight or Pencil Skirt

Before you begin, review Chapter 7 on designing your own straight skirt and designing your own A-line skirt. After reviewing these sections, you have a few decisions to make:

- What waistline treatment is on the A-line skirt? Do you want the same treatment on the straight skirt?

- What length is the A-line skirt? Do you want the same length on the straight skirt?

- Where is the zipper, if there is one? If the zipper is in the back seam, the process will be easier. If it's in the side, you may want to move it to the back. Depending on your patience and skill level, this could either be fun or a challenge! (See Chapter 2 for more on zippers.)

- In which seam do you want the kick pleat or slit? The best place is the back seam. Your A-line skirt may not have a back seam.

The simplest case:

- An easy-to-remove waistband; you may need to put in darts for the tummy and derriere.

- The zipper in the center back seam.

- Not a great deal of fullness (design ease) around the hips. Straight/pencil skirts tend not to have much design ease.

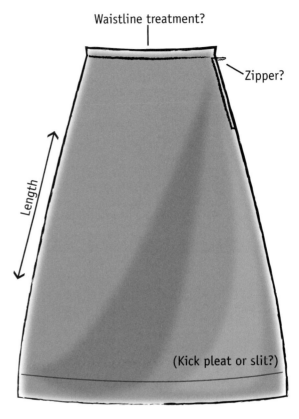

Converting an A-line to a pencil skirt

INSTRUCTIONS

1 Following the suggestions in Chapter 7, make a pattern for a straight skirt that will fit you. The side seams on a pencil skirt curve in slightly starting just below the widest part of your body, probably just around your hip line. The amount you curve in is entirely up to you, but don't forget to allow room for your thighs.

2 Lay the A-line skirt inside out on a table. Lay the pattern pieces made in Step 1. This will give you an idea of how much you will have to change. You may need to add some darts. You may need to make the hip measurement smaller.

3 If you have to make darts, carefully remove the waistband.

4 Allowing for the darts, if any, trace the straight pattern onto the A-line skirt, matching center fronts and backs, and the waistline. Don't forget to add seam allowances. Cut out the skirt.

5 Sew in the darts, sew the side seams, and replace the waistband. Undo the center back seam at the hem. The length will depend on how short the skirt is. If it's long, the slit will have to reach to slightly above the knees for walking.

6 If you have cut off the hem, rehem.

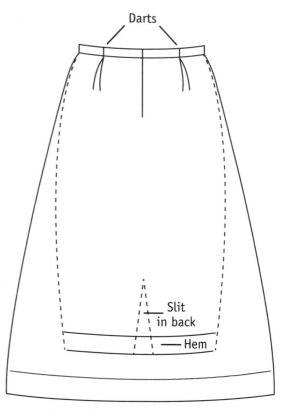

Converting an A-line to a pencil skirt

Fix a Hem

Why is it always just as you're ready to leave the house that you discover that the hem on the dress, skirt, or pants you want to wear has come undone? Don't worry! Fixing a hem is one of the easiest repairing tasks.

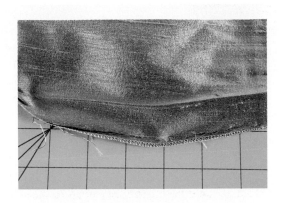

SLIPSTITCH

If the distance that the stitches have come out of the hem is less than 4 inches and the hem had originally been put in by hand with the stitches not showing on the right (public) side of the garment, you can slip-stitch the hem back into place. Be sure to make your stitches small enough that they don't show on the right side. (See Chapter 2 for techniques on slipstitching.)

IRON

If you have easy access to an iron, use one of the double-sided fusible web products that are designed for putting up hems. Note that these tapes don't work well on fabric with a high pile, such as velvet, or on a fabric that can't tolerate moisture, such as acetate. (See Chapter 5 for information on how to use the fusible web for a fused hem.)

GLUE

Fabric-friendly glues can help you repair your hem in a hurry. Read the directions on the bottle or tube for instructions specific to your particular fabric. If you will wash the garment often, sew the hem in place either by hand or on a sewing machine when you get time later.

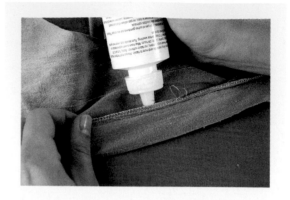

TOPSTITCH

If the hem that needs to be resewn is a topstitched hem, use a matching thread and topstitch the part of the hem that needs to be restitched, lining the stitching up with the previous stitches.

TIP

For a neater and less-noticeable hem, don't backstitch where you start and stop the stitching; instead, when you finish sewing, leave thread tails of about 4 inches. Then from the wrong side, pull up on the thread tail to pull the front thread tail through to the back enough to form a little thread loop. Insert a pin in the loop and pull the thread tail from the front side through to the wrong side and tie the two threads in a double knot.

Resew a Seam

If the stitches of a seam have simply come undone, you're in luck. All you need to do is sew the seam back together on your machine or by hand. If, however, the fabric itself has torn or raveled back near a seam, don't worry—a little more effort still likely can fix the problem.

REPAIR SEAM STITCH ONLY

If the stitches of a seam have simply come undone, start sewing an inch or so before the place where the stitches have come apart, and continue until about an inch into the part where the seam is still holding together.

Secure this old stitching by stitching over it and back-stitching. You can also hand-sew the seam back together using small backstitches. Trim all the threads.

REPAIR BOTH A SEAM AND TORN FABRIC

If the fabric itself has worn a hole, torn, or raveled back near a seam, and there is plenty of fabric in the damaged area, resew the seam by stitching the seam a little deeper so that the tear is now in the seam allowance rather than the garment.

NOTE: Remember that this will make the garment slightly smaller (tighter) in that area.

Mend Tears and Holes

How you fix a tear or hole is up to you and largely depends on where it is and its size and/or dimensions. You can patch with an appliqué or matching fabric, or you can darn a hole or embroider over a tear.

Patch the Tear

If the tear is in a place where no one will see it or it won't be obvious, use the patch method. You can put a patch on the wrong side of a tear to make the tear invisible—or nearly so. You also can put a patch on the right side that functions as a decorative embellishment as well as a solution to a problem.

PATCH WITH AN APPLIQUÉ

If the tear is on a leg or on the front of a top/jacket, choosing an interesting sew-on appliqué can be both functional and decorative.

Many iron-on patches are available in most stores that sell fabric notions. Some grocery stores even sell them. Just follow the directions that come with the patch. If you are going to wash the garment regularly, reinforce the edge of the patch with zigzag, decorative, or hand stitches.

PATCH WITH MATCHING FABRIC

If you can find a piece of fabric that matches the garment—for example, from the hem or facing, follow these steps to repair the tear or hole:

1 Trim the hole neatly, preferably into a square or rectangle.

2 Snip the corners of the hole diagonally ¼ to ⅜ inch, and turn all the edges under.

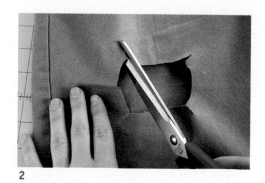

2

③ Cut a patch 1 inch larger than the hole, all the way around.

④ Press the edges of the patch to the right side.

⑤ On the wrong side of the hole, place the patch right side down and baste in place.

⑥ From the right side, turn the raw edges of the fabric to the inside and slip-stitch in place.

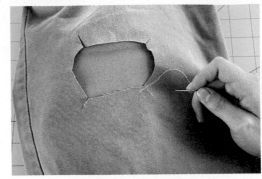

5

Darn a Hole

If the hole is small, it can be darned either by hand or by using the sewing machine. (Check to see if your sewing machine has a preprogrammed darning stitch.) It helps to do hand darning if you have a darning mushroom, darning egg, or some other smooth, round object that will keep the hole spread open and smooth while you weave the stitches.

① Using thread that is the same weight and color as the garment, sew a line of small running stitches around the hole. Be sure to catch fabric that is secure and solid.

② Sew a series of closely placed stitches parallel to each other across the tear or hole. Be sure to catch the running stitch you made earlier on each end. (Contrasting thread is used in the illustration for better visibility.)

③ When you have enough parallel stitches in one direction to completely cover the hole, turn the garment 90 degrees and begin to weave your stitches as if you were working on a weaving loom, going in and out of alternate rows of stitching.

Do not pull the stitches too tight or allow them to be too loose. Also, be sure to catch the earlier running stitches as you weave. The running stitches act as an anchor, especially on fabric that has been weakened.

NOTE: This is also how you would darn a hole in the heel or toe of a sock, using darning cotton thread.

Embroider Over a Tear

If you have embroidery stitches on your sewing machine, you may also be able to cover a small tear with an embroidery design, thus making the repair of the tear a design element. Again, it depends where the tear is. If the fix is going to be obvious to observers, embroidering over the tear is a good choice. You may even want to use the same embroidery stitches on other areas of the garment where there is no tear to balance out the design. This photo shows an embroidered stitch with bobbin thread (a less-bulky thread suitable for lightweight fabrics) and the same stitch with regular thread (for general use).

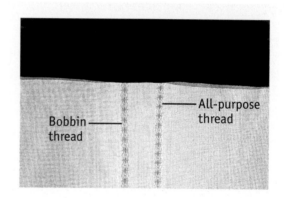

Bobbin thread

All-purpose thread

ockets are not purses or backpacks. Sometimes, however, we or those we love carry so much stuff in our pockets that the garment fabric wears through. Next thing we know, we are losing nickels and dimes. Here are some tips for what you can do when pocket problems arise.

PATCH POCKETS

- Patch pockets sometimes come unstitched, particularly on the upper corners. If the patch pocket was topstitched on, then, with matching thread, restitch the area that has come unstitched, matching up your stitching with the previous line of stitching.

- If it is the top of the pocket that has come out, make sure to backstitch to stabilize that area and prevent it from coming out again.

- If the patch pocket was sewn down orginally by hand, restitch that area of the pocket with an invisible hand stitch. (See Chapter 2 for hand-stitch details.)

- Take the opportunity to replace the patch pockets with some new ones in your choice of fabric. Have fun with this!

HOLES IN POCKETS

- Sometimes with wear and tear, the bottoms of your pockets may develop holes or come unstitched. If they are inseam pockets that simply come unstitched, then (from the wrong side of the garment) lay the pocket flat and restitch it.

- If the pocket is fairly deep and has a hole near the bottom, you can simply stitch a new bottom line of the pocket above the hole.

- If the pockets are not deep enough to shorten them by stitching a new line, then either fuse an iron-on patch or sew a patch on the hole by hand.

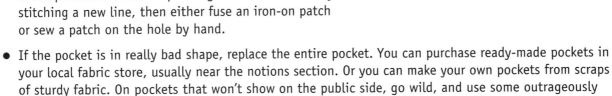

- If the pocket is in really bad shape, replace the entire pocket. You can purchase ready-made pockets in your local fabric store, usually near the notions section. Or you can make your own pockets from scraps of sturdy fabric. On pockets that won't show on the public side, go wild, and use some outrageously FAB fabric.

If you don't have one already, start your button collection now. Get a big jar and leave it in a handy place. When you purchase new clothes with buttons, you often find an extra button or two attached to the label or near the bottom hem. Put the extra buttons in your button jar. Also, before you turn an old blouse into a dust rag, cut off the buttons (particularly if they are distinctive or unusual) and put them in your button jar.

If you're lucky, you will have a button to match the button that needs replacing. Remove any old threads that remain where the button fell off. If the holes in the fabric are still obvious and the garment under the button is still intact, simply sew the button back on. (See Chapter 2 for more information on buttons.)

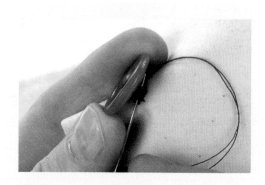

If you can't see the old holes, button up the garment and mark where the missing button belongs by sticking a pin through the buttonhole where the button is missing to mark the spot. Then sew on the button.

Sometimes the fabric under a button tears. If the button is still attached, carefully cut off the button, leaving as much fabric viable as possible. Carefully reinforce the tear by hand- or machine-stitching back and forth to darn a small area that will be hidden under the button. Then replace the button.

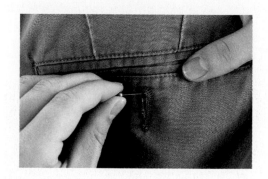

The weakest part of a buttonhole is at the ends. If there is a great deal of stress on the button and the buttonhole (as in this photo), the end will break and the buttonhole will become bigger and bigger. Result? Your pants will keep coming unfastened.

When (or, better, *before*) this starts to happen, do the following:

1. On the wrong side, reinforce the end of the buttonhole with a small piece of repairing tape extending into the buttonhole.

2. Very carefully hand-stitch several small stitches across the end of the buttonhole with matching thread. Be sure to catch the underneath tape in the stitches.

3. Cut the tape in the buttonhole to the original buttonhole size.

TIP

Replacing or repairing snaps, and hooks and eyes

If an end comes loose on a snap, hook, or eye, it can be restitched by hand (see Chapter 2). If you lose one part of the snap, hook, or eye, or if the snap, hook, or eye becomes bent out of shape, you can carefully cut the stitches holding it on and remove it. Mark the spot where it was stitched and cut away any excess thread. Then replace whatever is missing with the same size part. Always keep a supply of extra snaps, hooks, and eyes to make quick repairs whenever necessary.

Index

Notes

Notes

Yearning to do more with yarn?

Packed with photos, patterns, and step-by-step instructions,
you'll love knitting the visual way!

978-0-470-27896-3   978-0-470-07782-5   978-0-470-06817-5